AMMO GRRRLL IS HOME ON THE RANGE

Volume 4   2017-18

By SUSAN VASS

ISBN: 978-1-7327370-8-2

Published by VWAM, LLC, October, 2018

DEDICATION

To Samuel Colt (1814-1862), and William B. Ruger (1916-2002), makers of The Peacemaker, and my very first gun, the Ruger .22, respectively. These are just two of the many inventors, entrepreneurs, gunsmiths and geniuses who have afforded us the means to defend our homes and persons, as well as preserve our liberty. All other rights in this great and good land flow from our Second Amendment rights to keep and bear arms. Praise the Lord and pass the ammunition.

ANOTHER DEDICATION

THANKS BE TO:

The many faithful commenters and fans of my column, Thoughts from the Ammo Line, featured every Friday on the center-right on-line opinion site Power Line. These commenters are really now too numerous to mention by name. You know who you are and I love you all.

Special thanks as always to the Four Horsemen Helping Stave Off the Apocalypse with that site: Paul Mirengoff, John Hinderaker, Steve Hayward, and my excellent editor and friend, Scott Johnson.

Thanks also to my dear husband, Joe, who writes great novels under the awesome pseudonym, Max Cossack. Please buy his books for pure entertainment value, but then buy this book in yet more mass quantity so that I can come in first in our sales competition and win the bet on who has to do dishes for a month. Thank you.

WHO THE HECK IS AMMO GRRRLL AND WHY SHOULD I CARE?

After several decades as a standup comic, I retired and moved permanently -- from Minnesota – where I had to go away for several months in the frigid winter -- to Arizona, where I have to go away for several months in the hellish summer. Sadly, in this great and good land, if you happen to find a place with pleasant year-round weather, you can't possibly afford to actually live there.

Joe (Max Cossack – who writes novels which can be located and ordered on Amazon – did I mention that?) took up target shooting with a nice Springfield Armory .40 caliber pistol. At first, he could just go down to the local Walmart and buy boxes of ammo right off the shelves. But then Barack Hussein Obama became President and suddenly, ammo just dried up. I'm sure it was mostly a coincidence and had nothing to do with the bizarre idea that the Department of Agriculture, to name just one government agency, should have its own SWAT Team and millions of rounds of ammo. Whatever. He's gone now; and at this writing, Donald J. Trump is President and the shelves are once more full of ammo in nice organized stacks.

With ammo in short supply, it became my task to stand in line for many hours a day to secure it. This became a Sacred Quest and a social event and I acquired the nickname "Ammo Grrrll" from the sales people and other customers in line. This continued for a couple of years. Eventually, in March of 2014, I wrote what was a moderately-amusing little column about my experiences in gun-friendly Arizona and fired it off to Scott Johnson, of Power Line to see if he might be interested in a featured piece about the topic every once in a while.

Before I could even go get another cup of coffee, it appeared on the site and -- just like that! -- I was a columnist! It looked like I was never going to have to "Learn to Code" after all! True, there was no money in it, but, fortunately, my husband (Max Cossack, the famous novelist), had already Learned to Code and had done pretty well with it.

I could afford to be a Kept Woman, if you count doing cooking, cleanup, laundry, shopping, and housekeeping for about half a century being "Kept". Having two jobs with the column provides a kind of safety valve for my legendary and professional-level Powers of Procrastination. When I am "supposed" to be writing, I can decide that it is urgent to organize my sock drawer; and when I am "supposed" to be making and freezing appetizers for an upcoming cocktail party, I can tell myself that I better sit down at my computer and write a topical piece about the 29th Democrat candidate for President in 2020 – this one a trans-gendered Samoan who is also 1/1024th Navajo and can prove it with her application to law school in Colorado.

Then, I can actually do neither and just sit and read the newest Lee Child or Robert Crais book and pretend Reacher or Joe Pike is a very special friend of mine. Very special.

THE CONTEXT

The first column in "Ammo Grrrll Is Home On the Range" (Volume 4), makes its appearance on March 31, 2017. All "Ammo Grrrll Years" run from late March to late March due to the fact that my very first column appeared at that time.

The last column in the book appeared on March 30, 2018, probably just about a year ago, if my publishing schedule works out.

If you remember the little subheads in your American History Books in high school, you might remember such "eras" as "The Era of Good Feeling", "Tippecanoe and Tyler, too" or "The Era of the Insane Idea that Human Beings Could Be Chattel Slaves and That Would Turn Out Well."

March 2017 to March 2018 could most accurately be termed "The Era of Losing Losers' Hair on Fire as They Try to Overturn the 2016 Election".

EVERYTHING was a crisis, even though you probably can't name three of the crises without Google or Siri or Alexa or any of the other helpful reminders of the Media-Manufactured Crisis du Jour.

Oh. Em. Gee! President Trump had TWO scoops of ice cream at a banquet when his guests had only one! Yes! It's true, you guys! The Wacky Christian Vice President doesn't eat meals in public alone with a woman other than his wife! The Christmas decorations at the White House are too white! You get the idea…and you approve, if your emotional maturity ended in junior high, as we called it in my day.

You'll see what I mean about "hair on fire". Just turn the pages and reminisce. Enjoy.

APRIL, MAY, JUNE

The first quarter of the New Ammo Grrrll Year features a really wide spectrum of topics which would almost qualify as being "diverse", if diverse hadn't come to mean "a whole bunch of skin colors, sexual orientations, and genders with exactly the same opinions, monitored daily by the Thought Police and changed at a whim."

But "diverse" they are. My column topics begin with such things as feminists complaining that men are claiming too MUCH credit for sexually pleasing women. Which morphs seamlessly into a discussion of the Vice President's policy of not dining out alone with women to whom he is not married. Whoa, doggies! Veritable hair bonfires over that travesty!

There's a nice little piece addressing cultural food appropriation and the fun I had feeding matzo to my Mexican housekeeper and her son. Followed by a ludicrous "Listicle" in which the Most Beautiful Women List put Hillary Rodham Clinton at #6. In the world. You betcha. The week after that we talk about some of our hipper fellow citizens being willing to pay $425 for a pair of dirty jeans.

In mid-May, the column turns to such things as the ever-escalating demands of the "Oppressed" and the ever-expanding categories of such entitled humans; the obstacles from what is ostensibly "our" side to President Trump's urgent agenda; a little digression about all the Nanny State warnings on yet another of my road trips; and some alleged fisticuffs (or at least shoving) in the Montana election contest.

From there – Glory Be! – a recap on our family's history of modest wedding ceremonies on the occasion of our son's nuptials at a Twins double-header, and finally, the first "quarter" of the "Ammo Grrrll Year" comes to a close with a

6

column about the absurd hijacking by the violent fascist left of the "resistance" label, and another about the equally-absurd notion that cheating does not go on in elections. Which is exactly why they will fight to the death to prevent any kind of Voter ID. Read and enjoy them all.

LETTING UP

March 31, 2017

Being back in Minnesota in the winter has reminded me of a unique Minnesota expression of resilience and optimism. When you make plans to go out for the evening with a Minnesotan, by God, you're going! There can be a whiteout blizzard, you cannot see your hand in front of your face, and you call your friend to say "Do you think we should maybe, possibly rethink this outing?," and a true Minnesotan will say, "I think it's letting up."

No. It isn't. But you are not going to be able to wuss out without severe loss of face. Latin men may have reputations for machismo, but they have nothing on Minnesotans of any ethnicity in the winter, trust me, and that includes their womenfolk.

Now, watch carefully what I do here to segue into an entirely different subject:

I'll tell you another thing that isn't "letting up" and that's the mass hysteria over the election and its alleged dreadful consequences to various and sundry "oppressed" groups.

(See? That was a professional at work. Do Not Try This At Home!)

We've had actors hectoring the newly elected Vice President of the United States from the stage in a lapse of theatrical tradition and manners so egregious there's really no word for it. We've had an "important" film actor deliver a broadside

8

against the President when she was accepting yet another self-congratulatory award. That started quite the trend where it seemed that the sole purpose of the awards shows was for one sheep after another to try to out-bleat the last idiot with obscene or threatening criticism of the President.

We've had riots. We've survived two "general" strikes that claimed to show the horrors of a day without an immigrant and a day without a woman, though they looked to most of us clueless Deplorables like pretty unremarkable, yea, good days. We've had thousands of women walking around with strange little pink knit caps representing lady bits, though frankly, the resemblance was lost on me, along with the point.

Though I haven't watched it in many decades, John has reported that Saturday Night Live is devoting its meager comedic talents to full-time Trump-bashing now. The new wrinkle is that these brain-dead young writers, who couldn't think up one sketch critical of Obama in eight endless years, find it hilarious to have a woman playing a man from the Trump Administration. Whoa! Talk about side-splitting! Move over, Benny Hill.

It would be merely pathetic had not one charmless left-liberal used SNL as a springboard to become a United States Senator. After his performance in the Gorsuch hearings, if television ever remakes Perry Mason again, Senator Al Franken will be well-positioned to play Hamilton Burger, the lame district attorney who, in nine years, lost all but one case against Mr. Mason. (And somehow kept his job! Ah, government work!)

Sadly, Al's partner in partisan mediocrity, Senator Amy Klobuchar, who, rumor has it, is an actual attorney, gave too embarrassing a performance even to play a bailiff. It's always impressive to be reminded by mental midgets that the 18th Century geniuses who wrote the seminal documents of our great Republic, neglected to use politically-correct pronouns, like "xe". Never mind that there isn't a language at least of the five besides English that I have studied – Spanish, French, Latin, Hebrew, Russian – that doesn't use the masculine when referring to groups that include both sexes.

Space considerations compel me to offer but one final example of things not "letting up." When I was back in Minnesota, "up north" to visit my Papa, I had to stay in a hotel, what with the ol' family homestead sold and all. In the hotel breakfast room every morning, even though the television was routinely tuned to Fox News, the wretched Star Tribune was on the tables. I picked up the March 11 Variety section, thinking that would be my best bet at not having my head explode all over my Cheerios. Haha. As if. Sports, entertainment, nothing is safe.

Here is the opening paragraph of a fatuous article many column inches long about poems on the theme of "migration," and no, they aren't talking about birds going south for the winter: "Desperate times call for desperate measures. And really desperate times call for poetry." The gist of the article is that since the election, the fear and loathing abroad in the land has stimulated a renewed interest in poetry as a propaganda tool. Mostly because poems are short. Seriously. They prefer stuff that can be Tweeted.

Ah, yes. To return to my Minnesota roots: "You betcha." We live in "desperate" times: The people who soldiered on at home and abroad in two world wars, the people who survived the concentration camps to go on to establish the State of Israel, the millions who weathered a decade of soul-grinding poverty in the Depression, they had no idea what suffering was. It takes an election that doesn't go your way to really "get" what "desperation" is.

And having reached that point of existential despair, what could possibly help more than some pedantic free verse? I offer a poem of my own. It is short; rhyming, no extra charge.

Violets are nice, but Roses are best. Could you play with your Play Doh? And give it a rest?
Violets are blue. Roses are red. The Left has gone bonkers. And satire is dead.

XXX-TRA CREDIT

April 7, 2017

My astute, hard-working colleagues at Power Line are covering the Susan Rice disgrace and all the other important issues of the day. That frees me up to deal with the Left's Continuing Nervous Breakdown. The latest flapdoodle in Feminist Psycho Ninny World is whether or not men just get too darn much credit for giving women sexual pleasure, thereby somehow "hijacking" women's orgasms for themselves. Or something. The logic was hard to follow. Me, I'll take all the pleasure I can get without worrying about credit, but obviously I don't know what's important.

What I really worry about, and think should be looked into every day for many, many months, is whether or not the Russians are hijacking our orgasms.

Now, for a great many of the bitter feminists I have known, they could recuse themselves from the entire subject of sex with a man. In fact, many are so relentlessly enraged and unpleasant that I would speculate that what few miserable sexual experiences they have had at all have been alone. I know several sane, sweet lesbians who wouldn't be interested in that level of rage and negativity any more than a man would. Woohoo, Angry Ladies! You can claim ALL the credit for your orgasms. No sharing credit! You probably don't share entrees in Chinese restaurants either.

You would think that having a really great time in bed with a man would create a warm feeling of mutual accomplishment or even — dare I say it? — GRATITUDE. But no. NOTHING men do can ever be acknowledged as good. If a feminist asks a man a question and he answers as best he can, he is "mansplaining". This is bad, and needs to be called out.

Mr. AG has given up on mansplaining how to run the new Blu-Ray DVD player, use the dozens of remotes that seem to reproduce like bunnies, or make my computer behave, because he knows I won't be listening. I don't want to know HOW to do it, I want HIM to do it. And in return, I promise not to explain to him how to make perfect Brisket or Coconut Cream Pie. Which includes mile-high Meringue! (The pie, not the brisket.)

If several large, strong hunters sit next to you on a little plane headed for Billings, MT a few days after 9/11, a terrified comic could feel great relief and appreciation at being surrounded by a ton of patriotic testosterone. OR, she could feel that these big guys just take up too much room and are "manspreading." Another bad thing! And let's not even get into the horror of one of the men volunteering to put the vertically-challenged comic's carry-on into the overhead. Sexist beast!

Naturally, morally-superior women have never once sat their shopping bags on the seat next to them on the subway or a carry-on bag on each seat on either side of them in a crowded airport boarding area. And no women are 100 lbs. overweight and taking up inordinate amounts of space on the plane. Only men ever take up too much space.

So back once again to the current crisis of men getting too much credit for our orgasms. Back in the day when I worked with the 80 guys on night shift, a joke went around the shop that made me laugh out loud. It went like this: Question: "Why don't women have orgasms?" Answer: "Who cares?"

That was more than forty years ago. Evidently, the joke notwithstanding, both men and women DID care if women were having a good time in bed, if only because if women are enjoying themselves in bed, they may be inclined to go there more often.

So millions of column inches of words were spent 'splaining what might help to increase the chances that the ladies men slept with would have a more satisfying experience. *Cosmo* alone devoted every single article decade after decade to techniques and practices that were every bit as explicit as *Men's Health*, *GQ*, or even *Penthouse*. And, if all those noisy, sweaty romantic movies are to be believed, things improved.

Cause for celebration? Certainly not! We can't have happiness between men and women, in bed or out, can we? That spoils the narrative. So of course men are now getting blamed again. Blamed for not being good enough and blamed for being so good that they take pride in their contribution to women's happiness and fulfillment. That sounds about right: Heads, men lose; tails, women win. Tedious, but never surprising.

THE PENCE PROTECTION PRINCIPLE

April 14, 2017

If, like me, you are fortunate enough to live into late, late middle age, you will think that you have heard everything. But, sadly, you will have not.

So, when the breaking news story about Vice President Pence's principle of not dining alone with a woman other than his wife hit the airwaves, it could have triggered any number of sane reactions: "Oh, how interesting!" or "My, I wish my spouse would have followed that rule before he ran off with his accountant's secretary" or "That seems kind of old-fashioned and silly to me, but hats off to someone who takes no chances and puts his family first."

I have spent a lot of time around Lubavitcher Chasidim (so-called ultra-Orthodox Jews), who do not sit next to, be in a room together with a closed door, or even shake hands with people of the opposite sex. So the Vice President's principles did not strike me as unusual or particularly extreme, even though I have personally taken hundreds of meals alone with male friends, colleagues, and business clients.

But you can see why it would upset Democrats. They inhabit a world in which a kinda-sorta married ex-President flies off on a private plane called "The Lolita" to a private island of underage girls. They are not shocked when Hillary's galpal's husband sends repulsive pictures of himself in his Underoos to teenage girls while lying in bed with his toddler. Clearly, in Democrat World, the bar for decent behavior is set too low for even the most skilled limbo dancer to navigate.

So along comes a very intelligent, religious man who just says "No." And the commentariat explodes with the usual unhinged criticism of someone who had the audacity to own a principle. Besides the utterly predictable charges of sexism and bigotry, an employment attorney asserted that not dining alone with a woman could "harm the professional development of women." Oh, cry me a river! Find another way to "develop," ladies. Maybe, oh, I don't know, just by being extremely competent, loyal, smart, and indispensable?

And then this same employment attorney speculated that it could possibly even be ILLEGAL not to dine with women if you dine with men. Oh, please, by all means, bring that case to the Supreme Court. COMPULSORY dinner dates with women for married men! Find the shadow of THAT penumbra, Supremes!

Now apart from a precaution against his own ungoverned impulses, can we possibly think of another reason why Vice President Pence might avoid mixed groups who are drinking? Let's think real hard.

Good Lord, have none of these idiots ever watched a single episode of *West Wing* or *House of Cards*? ALL these self-important power junkies do night and day, is plot how to screw each other over. But, until they can accomplish that, they will settle for just plain screwing. Have you ever seen a character of any gender on either show that you could imagine trusting for five minutes with either your spouse or some personal confidence? Are you daft?

Let me give you just a couple examples of bad behavior I have witnessed personally where men, women and alcohol were involved. Because I am the cheapest date on the planet, who gets drunkish on half a martini, I will stipulate that it is possible that I have said a stupid thing or two under the influence myself. If you never have, congrats, and more power to ya!

Mr. AG and I were out for drinks with another couple at a prominent jazz club in the Twin Cities. A friend joined us at our table. And although I hoped I was mistaken, I distinctly heard the other wife say to our friend the minute he sat down, "I'm not wearing any underwear." Style points for subtlety to be sure, yet not too understated to be missed. Our friend at the time was a single, enthusiastic heterosexual who found this opening conversational gambit unusual, but not unwelcome.

We later learned that this damaged woman was in long-term therapy for routine behavior of this nature. Everyone around her was used to it and they just said, "Oh, that's just our Henrietta" (not her real name) and carried on as if nothing had happened.

At a jam-packed New Year's Eve party with a lot of people in "the arts," this same woman wedged herself in on the sofa next to Mr. AG and rested her hand on his thigh – with me sitting on a chair across from him! – until he rather pointedly got up and moved to the piano bench where he figured he was safe, at least while playing. Mr. AG was and is pretty attractive so, hey, I guess she was only human. The bizarre thing was that, apart from coming on to every man in the room, "Henrietta" was a perfectly-nice person.

Does the Vice President of the United States need crap like this? Because anyone crazy enough to tell a complete stranger that she was nekkid beneath her leather mini skirt is sure to be crazy enough to assert that HE made an inappropriate remark or otherwise assaulted HER. And then, who will the completely-unbiased media be eager to believe? Remember, women never lie. Only poor President Clinton had the bad luck to maul only liars. The odds against that had to be astronomical.

In the toxic, degenerate "gotcha" culture that is Washington, DC, the Pence Principle would be as much for protection from lawfare and blackmail as it would be from one's own baser instincts. Stick to your guns, Mike! Karen is a lucky lady who, God willing, will make a great First Lady in a short eight years.

LEFTIST LOONS SAY: NO MORE ETHNIC FOODS FOR YOU

April 21, 2017

Every week I make lunch or brunch for Anna, my cleaning woman, depending on her schedule. Being a Jewish mother, I believe it's borderline criminal to make anyone go more than four hours without eating. Three is better yet, just to be on the safe side. Anna works very hard, is the best housekeeper I have ever had, and I enjoy feeding her. She often brings her little 6th grade boy, Pedro, one of the lights of my life. Smart as a whip, completely bilingual, polite and well-behaved, he is a treasure among children.

She loves my cooking. (It is one of these six paltry skills/talents God gave me: typing, driving, shooting, cooking, speaking and writing amusingly about the passing scene, and, I have recently added "packing" – suitcases, not guns – in order to expand the list and feel better about myself. I once packed one small rollerboard that fit in the overhead for a twelve-day trip to Paris and Israel. Beat that, ladies.)

Anyway, not once has Anna worried either about my culturally appropriating the delicious treats she brings me or being served my Tuna Melt on Brooklyn Rye. But last week was problematic because we were still on Passover Dietary Rules and I didn't know what to feed her. Was it humane – or even legal? – to inflict matzo on a devout Catholic Latina?

I have a Passover staple dish called Minah de Pesach, which is a kind of cheeseless "lasagna" with a filling of

mushrooms, onions, chicken and eggs between layers of –
what else? – matzohs. This is paired with leftover charoset
from the Seder. Charoset is a singularly
unappealing-looking, but delicious concoction meant to
symbolize the mortar used for the bricks the Hebrew slaves
used. The version I have refined over many years is
finely-ground pecans and walnuts mixed with chopped
apples, raisins, dates, oranges, figs, currants, mashed
bananas and a little sweet wine. It is addictive and also
critical to give one's digestive system a little help in moving
along the concretized matzo.

Because Anna and her son know we are Jewish, they had
watched some new version of *The Ten
Commandments* show and had learned a great deal about
Passover. They were eager and proud to share what they
had learned about "Moises." Imagine that!

Both Anna and Pedro pronounced the food "delicious" and
said that they didn't think that matzo was all that different in
taste from flour tortillas. They gobbled up seconds, so I was
pretty sure they weren't just being polite.

The night before, they had been to a big quinceanera party
for a friend's beautiful young girl. They showed us pictures
and video from the event, complete with wonderful music
and dancing. Pedro is learning to play guitar and studied
with Mr. AG, a font of musical knowledge, for over two hours,
while Anna and I did our respective work.

To my mind, one of the great benefits of America's unique
and awesome Diversity has always been the back and forth
flow of food, recipes, music, dances, and other enriching
cross-cultural exchanges. My life would have been greatly
diminished without Chinese Potstickers, Indian Massamun
Curry, Vietnamese Eggroll, or even Enchiladas and Pizza.

Since Jews have lived in and then been exiled from so many countries, our cuisine is already a mishmash of nearly every great ethnic cuisine the world over. In the 8 days of the holiday this year, for example, I made Yemenite Chicken, a Yiddish Short Rib Stew called a Tzimmes (roughly translated as "yuge hassle"), Greek Salmon Patties and my own take on an Israeli Charoset. No kidding.

Even for your average American, in that same week he might have a pulled pork sammich originating from Puerto Rico, Tacos, and Spaghetti.

But our betters tell us we've been doing it all wrong! Eating the food of another culture is a grievous Sin of Cultural Appropriation. Of all the stupid stupidities that the stupid-heads of the Left have thought up, stupidly, this one takes the cake. (And God forbid that cake should be the Dobos Torte from Austria my late mother-in-law won a $50 prize for! Unlike Obama, she even spoke "Austrian," which is to say German.) And proves once again, how short-sighted and STUPID these people are. Can you imagine ANY ethnic restaurant surviving on only the clientele that matches its ethnicity? Do Leftists care if an Indian or Thai restaurant survives? "They" didn't build that; their Lightbringer Leader told them that.

If the Oberlin College cafeteria serves a mile-long buffet of ethnic food and you have to present your DNA analysis from Ancestry.com in order to be served your only genetically-sanctioned choice, what possible purpose has been served? How is enjoying a food "appropriating" it? Suppose someone does actually open the Thurston Howell Taco Emporium to compete with Albertos? The marketplace will sort it out right quick. I don't know who gets to eat good 'ol American hamburgers or Tuna Casserole. Are Mexican or Chinese students forbidden from that or, as with virtually all "diversity," do all privileges flow only one way? (They can eat "our" food; we just can't eat "theirs"? Sounds par for the course.)

When Anna and Pedro were leaving, I heard him speak in rapid Spanish to his mother in which I recognized the word *"pan"* (bread). Anna shook her head, but I asked him in English if he wanted some more of the matzo "candy" he had enjoyed. (A layer of matzo, a layer of homemade toffee, and topped with melted chocolate and chopped nuts.) No. What he wanted was a few sheets of plain matzo, bless his little heart!

One of Mr. AG's and my favorite episodes of *Cheers* involved Henri, a French ladies' man winning a bet with Sam and yelling, "France wins! France wins!" to which Frasier comments drily, "THERE'S something you never hear." Mr. AG reprised the line: "May I have some plain matzo for the road?" "There's something you never hear." *Es verdad.*

PICTURE THIS

April 28, 2017

Hollywood and The Internet love lists and competitions. Every year People magazine crowns some man as "The Most Handsome Man in the World" and puts his picture on the cover. Sometimes I find the man reasonably attractive – though rarely armed and usually not manly or old enough for my taste – and sometimes I say out loud right there in the checkout line: "Are you kidding me? Mr. AG is much cuter than him!" Sometimes people behind me will move to another line even if there are elderly women in it with lots of coupons and checkbooks.

Now, a couple weeks ago, along comes a clickbait list from an outfit called Buzznet of the 30 Most Beautiful Women in the World. Yes! The whole world!

When I saw that Hillary Clinton had come in at #6 – in the world, remember! — I excitedly checked the rest of the list to see if I was on it. If Hillary was #6, it seemed equally likely that I had also made the cut! What a day-maker THAT would have been!

Alas, it was not to be. Which is probably just as well, as I understand that the paparazzi are a big problem for the very beautiful. And you aren't allowed to just shoot them (either the very beautiful OR the paparazzi). It turns out it isn't even legal to beat paparazzi up as some people have discovered too late.

Now I happen to believe that Hillary was a terrible candidate because she is a terrible person, with terrible ideas delivered in a terribly boring manner, but not because she is unattractive. I think she is a perfectly acceptable looking older woman, but for the love of Pete, she is NOT nohow, no way, the 6th most beautiful woman in the world.

In fact, looking around the supermarket in my Dusty Little Village the day that news came out, I saw at least ten "ordinary" women just pushing carts of carbs down the aisle who were much better looking than Hillary. And that supermarket was Walmart.

Walmart is not famous for beautiful women. The Internet routinely posts photographs of unfortunate-looking, inappropriately-clad Walmart shoppers for the amusement of mean people who like to feel superior to others, especially fat or poor people.

Mother Teresa and Eleanor Roosevelt were not pretty either, so what? Looks are not everything in life, but if that's what the list purports to rank, then looks are what should count. Not even to mention that there is a wide gap between the categories of "average," "cute," "pretty" and BEAUTIFUL. That's a very high bar.

If you want to make a list of "insanely-driven" women, or "influential women" or more accurately, "women who peddle influence," then Hillary could be placed high on those lists. But beautiful? Come ON. A list of "most beautiful" that puts Hillary on it and pointedly leaves off First Lady Melania is dishonest right out of the box. I know very little about Melania, but there is one darn good-looking woman.

So where do I think I might belong on a list of World's Most Beautiful Women? This will be a totally unscientific "ballpark" stab, my picky friends, recognizing that (1) there are lots of babies and children in the female population who wouldn't count as women and (2) I dropped Statistics in college because I was failing. Twice. Feel free to do your own math. If there are 7.5 billion people in the world, and half are female, and I consider myself "average," I may be the 1.87 billionth best-looking woman in the world. Give or take. Woohoo!! Talk about the ultimate Participation Trophy!

Of course, so much of that "competition" would be not just the babies and adolescents mentioned above, but all women unfairly younger than me. Once you limit the contest to the Late, Late, Middle Age category, I do considerably better. I have noticed that sometimes in restaurants, particularly all-you-can-eat buffets, I have achieved the coveted status of "Least Overweight Woman My Age in the Room".

So confining the pool just to Lady Baby Boomers, AND if I lost the last #@&* ten pounds I have lost at least forty times, I could move up many notches to, say, fifty-millionth best-looking woman. Though what possible difference that would make in my very happy, blessed life I cannot say. I know that with Carole Lombard deceased and Scarlett Johansson not available, that I am at least #6 on Mr. AG's list and that is enough for me.

I feel quite confident that with Buzznet's ideologically-driven list of 30 ladies, I can type faster and shoot more accurately than any of them. So I got that goin' for me, which is nice. Hopefully, I'm funnier too, except for Hilarious Hillary, who, as we saw on the campaign trail, brought the house down with that knee-slapper "Deplorable" routine. And who can forget: "Did you wipe your server?" "You mean, like, with a cloth?" Hooboy, that's comedy gold!

LITTLE NUGGETS OF JOY

May 5, 2017

Some weeks are harder than others. We learn of grave difficulties that friends and relatives are facing. Serious, heart-wrenching things. It would be easy to give in to despair when there is so much suffering, especially when the political climate is frustrating as well.

It's challenging to stay upbeat when an Obama-appointed bagman and judge says we taxpayers cannot punish flagrant, proud lawbreakers by cutting off their funds. Or when event after event with conservative speakers is either canceled or violently attacked. But despair is a dead end that leads to political impotence and further defeat. We must think of the Winter Soldiers of Valley Forge and find courage.

And never never lose our sense of humor. Humor is both a balm for us and our best weapon against the Left.

So it's important to look for little nuggets of joy. I'm here to help. Some random nuggets:

Like finding out that the psychotic monsters of the Islamic State (that has nothing to do with Islam) who were about to attack the Kurds were set upon and killed by – wait for it – wild boars. Yes, a SWAT team of jihadi-gobbling PIGS. Three dead; five wounded. For all you people not bound by Jewish dietary laws, please, for me, have a BLT in celebration.

Though perhaps EATING a pig may not be the most

appropriate response in this case, it does put me in mind of a great pig joke I include free of charge.

A traveling salesman ambles up the drive of a farm and sees a three-legged pig hopping about. He asks the farmer, "What's the story here?" The farmer says, "Well, that's a smart wonderful pig. He smelled smoke late one night, broke into the house and alerted us all to a fire. Saved our lives, that's for sure." "So, is that how he lost his leg, in the fire?" "Oh no, he was unscathed. But a pig that heroic, you can't eat a pig like that all at once."

Over the weekend, I put in my summer flowers – vincas – almost the only ones that can withstand Arizona's maximum 120-degree heat. Gardening in and of itself is a little nugget of joy, but that's not where I'm going with this.

The good news is that I got my jeans pretty dirty. Several Internet sites were recently abuzz with the forehead-smacking news that people are willing to pay Nordstrom up to $425 for dirty jeans. Ladies, or very short, genderfluid men, if you wear Size 6 jeans, I am willing to let mine go for HALF OF THAT!

BUT WAIT, THERE'S MORE: there is also an authentic Biscuits and Gravy stain – well, just the gravy, biscuits don't stain. AND there are three smallish, yet noticeable holes from clumsily-handled gun-cleaning solvent. It's a Red State trifecta! You can pretend to be a blue collar worker, a shooter and a person who eats Southern comfort food instead of arugula, all for the reasonable price of just $212.50.

Act before midnight, and I will even throw in an impressive blood stain on a nice white shirt from my gun range. No, nobody shot me at the range. I got into an unintentional dust-up with a cactus in my yard. Which I lost. Badly. You can pretend to be an antifa rioter and say, "You should see the OTHER guy."

Mr. AG has hundreds of grotesque old t-shirts with sweat stains so that you could pretend you lift weights or run, both of which he does, and both of which are a sweaty business in Arizona. Understand this about my dear husband, my friends. Nothing, and I do mean nothing, can be thrown away. Ever. So, back when dinosaurs roamed the earth, the running shirts were once navy blue or black, though most have now faded to a nondescript greyish blue that matches everything. A steal at $100 apiece and boy, will he be surprised when they are gone and I finally get my Ed Brown 1911!

This could open up a whole line of awesome products for poseurs or ironic hipsters. For example, for liberal women who would like to pretend that they have had sex with Bill Clinton without all the mess, fuss, kneepads and outsized ChapStick budget, Nordy's could come out with a line of pre-stained little blue dresses. Like the old Cabbage Patch dolls of yore that came with Adoption Papers, for just a little more, you could get a genuine fake Certificate of DNA.

NEVER ENOUGH

May 12, 2017

I knew a child many years ago, abandoned by her mother at a young age, who kept reliving that feeling of abandonment by constantly upping the ante in demands until she was told "No" and she could have a meltdown.

One day we went on a lovely outing to a local park and rode on the paddleboats on the lake; she asked to go to an amusement park, which we did. She asked for so many treats she got sick. She asked to ride on many rides until she came to one for which she did not make the height requirement. She went nuts. "Why didn't you say 'No' sooner, you ask?" I truly wanted to see exactly what it would take to make her happy. The answer: it couldn't be done. She was damaged. It became quite clear that she didn't ENJOY being happy.

Because most conservatives identify as responsible "grownups," and many leftists of either sex identify as spoiled, mean, high school girls, I think "progressive" politics has proceeded in a similar fashion. I could give ten examples; I will just use one today.

There are many conservatives who either have someone in their extended family or know someone who is gay. So, when gay couples wanted to have some kind of commitment ceremony, many conservatives attended such events. (In one case, my very redneck neighbor in Minnesota hosted a ceremony in his backyard for a lesbian friend. The stupid, made-up epithet "homophobic," like its cousin, "racist," is flung like poo by monkeys, but is generally a lazy, convenient lie or wild exaggeration.)

But very soon a "commitment ceremony" wasn't enough. We noticed that in our Reform synagogue the ancient words "husband and wife" were systematically getting replaced by the bland and meaningless "partner," preparatory to erasing all distinctions between marriage between a man and a woman and marriage between two people of the same sex. I thought it would take longer to undo thousands of years of culture and tradition. I was wrong. Things that take millenia to build can be destroyed in a heartbeat.

In 2000, there was a vote in ultra-blue California on same sex marriage. All the Right People backed it. Yet traditional marriage won handily. But the sore losers were relentless. Here comes 2008, the First Black President is about to win and he is thought to have broad coattails. Try, try again. Whoa! What's this? Black people, who turned out in record numbers, also believed – as the black candidate himself declared when asked – that "marriage" is between one man and one woman. Same sex marriage lost again.

Then one gay judge wiped out both large democratic votes in one fell swoop and promptly retired never to have to pay for a drink in a gay bar again. So much for the sanctity of "popular votes," eh, Hillary?

Though I worried about the slippery slope this monumental redefinition of a bedrock institution represented, this was not an issue that was on the front burner with me. For most people, "fairness" resonates keenly. I knew heterosexuals who divorced before they could get out their thank you notes for wedding gifts, and gay couples together for forty years.

You would think that the gays and the progressives would still be popping champagne, but again, you would be wrong. The poor losers turned out to be even more vicious winners.

They outed supporters of traditional marriage and hacked into databases and punished anyone who had dared to believe what Candidate Obama said he believed.

Since there is not a single argument for gay marriage — it's about "equality"; it's about simple fairness; it's just about "who you love" — that cannot also be applied to two men and a woman or three women and a Siamese Cat, the precedent has been set and the erosion of the institution will continue apace. As Rush would say, "Don't doubt me."

And now comes the ludicrous obsession with the Trans-gendered. The "rights" of this minuscule population of gender-confused or fad-driven humans to use any bathroom du jour they choose are suddenly of paramount importance! And damn the bigots who object to their little girls being forced to share a bathroom with a man in a dress who likes to ogle little girls.

Try even to imagine what "letter" could come after the "T" in the Grand Pecking Order of Entitlement. Twenty years ago did you ever dream that the MILITARY (taxpayers) would be forced to pay for Brad the Gay Male Traitor to transform physically into Chelsea the *Cause Celebre*? If only Benedict Arnold had thought to call himself Bernice and demand free surgical alteration instead of alteration of the length of his neck.

So I return to my opening theme: It's never enough; the Left will never cease adding categories of Entitled Victims, whose "rights" will supercede those of working people, normal people, religious people of any color, but for sure white people, especially white men.

Maybe, just maybe, once in a great while, there is a cost to forcing every degenerate or cockamamie policy down our throats.

Target president Brian Cornell, watching his cash flow in the opposite direction like the Bama football motto "Roll, Tide," has now **let it be known** that when the Insane Corporate Decision was made, he was in the now infamous Target bathroom, or something. Maybe he said he was out of town, whatever. In any event, he is trying to weasel out of responsibility for a corporate decision right up there with New Coke or running Hillary again.

No big deal to these corporate elites with their Golden Parachutes and stock options and grotesque salaries to start with. Even if he loses his job, he won't exactly be in the same shape as the victims of the "Woo-hoo! We're Gonna Kill Coal" campaign, will he? As they say in Coal Country, the choices for their sons are "coal mine, moonshine (now meth and oxy), or walk on down the line." Maybe if they agree to mine coal in a dress they will achieve protected status.

A RACKET WRIT LARGE

May 19, 2017

A book that had a profound effect on me as a teenager was *A Tree Grows in Brooklyn* by Betty Smith. Francie, the young protagonist, was, like me, a READER who discovers the library and it changes her life. Unlike Francie, however, we were middle-middle class, living in small towns in South Dakota and Minnesota, and Francie was starvation-level poor, living in a tenement in Brooklyn with a distant mother and a loving but hopelessly alcoholic father.

In the book, there is a neighborhood candy store, run by a fat, creepy child molester. (No, not Lena Dunham; this was in 1912.) He runs a "game" in which a little board has several covered squares with prizes behind them from penny candy to a gorgeous doll prominently displayed. The child can choose a square for a small sum, a nickel, if memory serves me. But nickels were very hard to come by. In all the time Francie plays, she never wins the doll or anything else of value, and only loses her precious coins.

She grows up, is a modest success, and returns to the candy store. She has a couple of dollars now and, in front of witnesses, buys every square on the whole board, over the strenuous objections of the crooked candy store operator. As even I had figured out as a kid, there was NO DOLL behind any of the squares. It was just a cruel racket.

I was put in mind of that racket when we Deplorables won the Presidency, the House and the Senate. We had run the table, bought all the squares on the card! Surely, Conservatism would now have its way draining the swamp!

Lucy can't pick up the football forever, can she? Can she? At some point, shouldn't Charlie Brown man up and just clock her? Oh, not with a bike lock or anything – that's just legal for antifa fighters against free speech – just enough of a whack that she maybe wouldn't do it again.

I do not expect miracles, especially in some silly artificial time limit like 100 days. But for the love of God where is the budget for The Wall? How are the bids going for the project? If money is "owed" to the criminal-protecting scofflaws in "sanctuary" cities or states, just don't write the checks. How hard is that? Make the judge-shoppers who shut that down try to enforce it.

Here's what I think: I think the main reason that dozens of self-serving, treacherous Republican elected officials lost their minds when the Deplorables got Trump the nomination was that they had no confidence that Trump understood how this giant con game was supposed to work.

Hillary was SUPPOSED to win; the Obama Third Term would roll on; and the Congresspeople and Senators for Life with a whimsical, meaningless "R" after their names would consort amiably with the D's, lining their pockets, feathering their nests, eating the famous Senate Bean Soup, never having to abide by the laws they passed, and clucking their teeth every two or six years about how they were prevented from DOING even one thing they promised because Hillary would just veto it. It's great to be a Minority Party with all of the perks and none of the responsibility. And a lifetime sinecure. Everybody wins but the conservative taxpayer. And anyone who loves America. But I repeat myself.

What real policy differences do John McCain, Paul Ryan, Lindsey Graham and those mealymouthed women I can never even keep straight (Lisa and Susan something?) actually have with Schumer and Pelosi? Please list the differences, ladies. We're all just supposed to be so gosh-darn happy that you have lady bits that we don't realize you are worse-than-useless turncoats always on the wrong side of every question?

If the Wall does not get built, if pretend refugees from terror-loving countries do not get properly vetted, if the "peace process" continues to mean taking more pieces from Israel, as God is my witness, I will never vote Republican again or give any money to buy another square behind which is just another liberal prize.

Except for the fact that I would vomit all over myself, why not just go over to The Dark Side? If you're a Democrat, you get to riot in a mask, burn down buildings, make fake rape charges, make fake hate crime charges, admit to child molestation in your own book, use many branches of the Federal Government to unlawfully harass and intimidate conservatives, advocate cop killing, shout down speakers, call for the murder of the President, and clap like a spastic seal at late-night comics making obscene jokes about the President of the United States. Jokes that would absolutely be deemed "homophobic" from any conservative.

Can you imagine any late-night host keeping his job after saying that Obama's mouth was a "holster" for the Ayatollah of Iran's wee-wee? Which, according to the new book about Barry, was not nearly as far-fetched.

And here's the great part: there are no consequences for any of it!! Consequences are for Life's Deplorable little losers.

USE EXTREME CAUTION!

May 26, 2017

No, my dear friends, that is not a warning which must be legally appended to the New York Times, Washington Post, or Red Star of the North Tribune, to prevent you from taking any information therein with anything but a grain of salt substitute.

I have recently been on yet another long road trip from Arizona back to Minnesota to see my elderly Papa. We have had a lovely week – going out for lunch and coffee, visiting friends, and watching a nightly movie once I get the DVD player set up, which rarely takes me more than half an hour.

Did I ever mention how many electronic and mechanical devices hate me on sight? When Anthony "Bawling Tony" Weiner's first creepy photos of himself went viral, his First Lie was that he had been "hacked" (sound familiar?) and he tweeted, "What's next? Attacked by my toaster?" Initially, I actually thought to myself, "Well, THAT could totally happen." I have had several unpleasant encounters with blenders, juicers and the like. But I digress…

Since I have made the cross-country journey multiple times in the 3-plus years of the column, I have shared most of the observations about this trek that there are to make. And yet, another column is due! So, here are a few more random thoughts:

Where the posted speed limit is concerned, most generally law-abiding Americans firmly believe that "7-10 miles over the posted limit" is what the sign-posters really meant. And they are very aggrieved if the Highway Patrol does not agree. This is universal, by the way, and cannot be corrected for obvious reasons: if you made the speed limit 120, people would believe that 127-130 should be fine. Ad infinitum.

In fact, it makes me wonder – what with this demonstrable and admirable anti-authoritarian streak in Americans – if we wouldn't be better off with an Autobahn situation with no speed limit at all. In many parts of Arizona, New Mexico and West Texas, the speed limit runs 75-80 mph, but I do not feel comfortable going 80, except when passing. I will tool along in the right-hand lane, with the Cruise Control set at 77. However, 77 is what I like to go even when the speed limit is 55. In the words of our Israeli cousin who has his own phone-book sized record of driving offenses, "This is how I go."

Thought Number Two (hardly the first to notice): We have become a Great Big Nanny State with warnings about everything. When exactly, did we become a nation whose drivers need to be told not to "drive into smoke and fire"? Was it before or after the lengthy list of warnings for a Dustbuster included "Do not vacuum up water?" and "Do not vacuum glowing cigarette ashes?"

I have also been reminded repeatedly on this journey not to pick up hitchhikers in the vicinity of prisons. Did somebody's brother-in-law own a lucrative road sign making company, or does the government think that a small, weak, elderly (though armed) woman alone will offer a ride to a lot of nervous men wearing orange jumpsuits?

I have mentioned before my great amusement at the enigmatic sign "Dust storms may exist" and its companion a few feet down the road, "Visibility may be zero." If visibility were zero, wouldn't that make both signs impossible to see, in which case, what was the point? The next sign is moderately useful: "Do not stop in the traffic lane." This is always good advice, dust storm or not. And bringing up the rear is "USE EXTREME CAUTION."

No, this is not a situation that calls for ordinary, garden-variety caution. Your caution should be extreme. What that entails is not made clear, other than not stopping in the traffic lane. You probably should just leave the freeway at the nearest exit and go back home. Lock your door, shove a hefty piece of furniture against it, grab a plush toy or Play-Doh and hide under your bed. In any event, something EXTREME.

This sign is quite an apt metaphor for the current political climate.

We have to use EXTREME CAUTION when expressing any mildly political opinion, lest we inadvertently commit a microaggression and lose our jobs. We have to use EXTREME CAUTION when sending our little boys to school, lest they bite a Pop-Tart or piece of bologna into the shape of a gun or, worse yet, point an index finger at another little boy and say "Bang." We Deplorables did that as children, and look at how terrible WE turned out: voting for Literally Hitler!

Use EXTREME CAUTION when ordering ice cream. Under no circumstances should you be caught having two scoops of ice cream when others have only one. This will result in a screen grab of the news crawl that will be beamed all over the world and to distant planets. This is what they now teach in journalism schools constitutes a "scoop."

Have a nice day. Unless you don't want to. I would never presume to try to define for you what a "nice day" even is. Maybe it's putting on a dress and going into the ladies' room if you were "assigned" male parts by the Cosmic Parts

Assigner, not to be confused with God. Maybe it's putting on an ISIS-chic little black outfit and starting something on fire. There are no bad ideas in Antifa World.

But whatever you do to make your day "nice," which is probably some way a racist word, because black people have a disparity of nice outcomes, the important thing is always and at all times to USE EXTREME CAUTION.

HOLD MY BEER!

June 2, 2017

One of my favorite jokes concerns several "famous last words" in Texas. Attributed both to Kinky Friedman and Jeff Foxworthy, prominent among these last words are "Watch this" and "Hold My Beer." Montana is fairly similar to Texas in outlook when some jackass gets in your face. It is one of my favorite states. Gunracks in pickups, and friendly guys who wave at a little woman out walking, what's not to like?

Come with me in the Wayback Machine to the early days of SNL. Remember when Bill Murray used to play a guy "reviewing" the nominated movies in advance of the Oscars, and he would admit to never having watched but one or two? That was funny and, of course, it didn't prevent his having an opinion on them.

So I will stipulate in advance that I have not watched any video of the "Thrillings in Billings" or the "Punch In the Nose, Man, in Boseman." Wherever. Further, I could not pick either combatant out of a police lineup. I know no more about the facts of the case than the entire media know about what would motivate Putin to rig the election in order to sabotage the careless crook who was giving out uranium in swag bags. But I do have an opinion.

The nasty, wretched, wussified loser Democrats just got beat – AGAIN – by Toxic Masculinity, long may it wave. Ha. Ha. And also Ha.

It may also have helped that there was considerable early voting, though I have read on Power Line that that is not the case. Nonetheless, as I surmised and hoped, sensible Montanans were not overly upset that their guy engaged in a little pushing and shoving or even "body-slamming" with a d**khead "reporter" from the anti-Semitic left-wing Guardian.

I suppose now would be a good time to make the obligatory disclaimer that I do not condone or engage in any body-slamming, except gently in the privacy of my own bedroom, and not in the political arena for sure. And also that these views do not reflect those of the Power Line Boys (except Scott on a really bad day), their wives, journalist children, or any of their sponsors or advertisers, or the advertisers' relatives or household help. But COME ON.

We have all seen a reporter ask "How do you feel right now?" to a (pick one): World Series losing pitcher who is crying; shell-shocked woman whose home has just been blown away by a tornado; or devastated little girl who has just lost the Little Miss Contest, while shoving a microphone and camera into his or her face.

Breathes there a man with soul so dead who never to himself has said, "That obnoxious, intrusive, misery-monger needs a good strong smack to the head"?

We have all seen a Presidential press conference of a Republican president in which, to take but one example, the late and unlamented Helen Thomas would screech the same "asked and answered" question about "murderous, overreacting Israelis" over and over again.

We have all read of 60 Minutes programs routinely interviewing their targets for hours and hours and then carefully editing all that footage to get exactly the "gotcha" spin they want. Sometimes even featuring an "answer" to a completely different question.

And that doesn't make you occasionally want to hit someone? No? Seriously? Well, you're a better man than I am, Gunga Din. But, I suspect most are. Before my rotator cuff injury, I used to fantasize about mud-wrestling Andrea Mitchell till that smug look was wiped off her face, or at least severely messing up her hair. Wouldn't you pay to watch that as a Power Line fundraiser? Heck, it would even be worth it if I lost.

A rather difficult woman at our former synagogue once complained to Mr. AG that our beloved rabbi had been horribly unrabbinical and had told her to shut up. And Mr. AG, in one of his habitual, endearing cross-examinations asked, "What did YOU say right before he said that?" Not only did she not answer his question, she literally never spoke to him again. (May she rest in peace now, however.)

The Left has done a heckuva LOT "before that." Our speakers are shouted down with impunity. And that's if they can even fight their way through the masked, ISIS-costumed, rioting antifas to a venue. If the sponsoring group has ponied up enough insurance (ransom) against the left's violence. For eight long years, the mildly conservative Fox News was attacked by the President and his lickspittles, who would tolerate nothing but cringe-worthy fawning.

And don't give me, "We're just as bad as they are if we engage in 'violence.'" No, we aren't. There really is such a thing as self-defense. As "Stand Your Ground." Every child over the age of five understands the injustice of moral equivalence when "He started it." They started it; they have been engaging in physical violence since long before the election. It's way past time to say, "Hold my beer."

MARRIAGE VS. WEDDINGS

June 9, 2017

I'm warning readers in advance that I might inadvertently be stepping on some toes today. Truly, I mean no disrespect. Please believe me that if you already had a big wedding, I hope you enjoyed every minute. If you are currently planning a wedding with 400 guests for a son or daughter, mazel tov and more power to you. We Jews are enjoined to "celebrate with the bride and groom" as a major mitzvah (commandment). It's all good.

All I'm saying is, if it had been up to our family, the wedding planners and whole gouging industry would have gone out of business long ago. Heck, my cousin had a Bride Doll when we were kids that I thought was the only toy more boring than Barbie. She (the cousin, not Barbie) had a giant Texas wedding with eight bridesmaids, their groomsman escorts, two flower girls and two ringbearers. The photographer could hardly get the whole wedding party in the picture without a crane shot. The marriage lasted about 15 years. Just sayin'.

My dear parents were married in the living room of Mama's small home in Astoria, South Dakota, when Daddy was home on leave from the Navy. When I took Mama to the town's 110-year reunion, I learned from a lady who had been about twelve at the time that she and her three littler sisters stood on tiptoe outside the window of the house to watch the ceremony. She told me that Mama and her sister were considered to be "almost movie stars" they were so pretty, and this little wedding was quite a thrill. As kind readers know, Mama died last year. She and Daddy had been married for 71 years.

Mr. AG and I eloped in June of 1967. (To Chelsea: Yes! I was a child bride because of global warming…) After the brief ceremony in Kalamazoo, Michigan (one of just three states then that would allow a man under 21 to get married without parental consent), we had a "reception" party back on campus at Northwestern that lasted about three days and eventually included celebrants we had never seen before in our lives.

My parents were in attendance for the first night and our hippie friends, forewarned not to antagonize my conservative father, wore their Bar Mitzvah or Confirmation suits and ties. With their long 1967 hair and beards, beads and headbands, they looked like modern versions of Centaurs – with the head of a hippie and the clothes of a Yuppie. A wrinkled, and mothball smelling Yuppie in tight jackets and very short pants in some cases. For those who might be math-challenged, that means we celebrated 50 years of marriage. Last week.

And now the tradition continues into the next generation. A couple of weeks ago, our son and his fiancee announced when we were back in Minnesota to get our house ready to sell that in 48 hours they were planning to get married in the 3rd inning of a double-header at Target Field. In a suite that held 24 people, later upgraded to 36. Luckily, I had just bought a cute little dress at Bass Pro in Texas on the way to Minnesota. Though Bass Pro is not famous for wedding attire, it sufficed. Sadly, there was no camo involved. The Mother of the Groom is traditionally supposed to "wear beige and keep her mouth shut." How much better then would it be for it to be impossible even to pick her out of the wedding pictures due to camouflage? We had great ballpark food. It was truly the most fun, relaxing wedding I have ever attended.

My beautiful new daughter-in-law said that she had friends

who were still paying off humongous wedding bills – after their divorces. She really didn't want to squander a lot of (anyone's) money on a one-day blow-out when they could put that money to a down payment on a new house or even a world-class honeymoon. She thought I would be upset. Mr. AG and I were both over-the-moon thrilled. The Twins did lose the first game of the double-header, however, but everything else was magnificent. They have already been married for 19 days.

In fairness to the Big Wedding advocates, I have read that some research indicates that those marriages last longer than smaller affairs. The article speculated that the arduous task of planning every detail together provided a foundation for future conflict resolution. I think most of the "conflict" is probably between the Bridezilla and her mother. An Internet list of 100 reasons it's great to be a guy featured at #28: "Wedding plans take care of themselves."

Two more recent trends that I find troublesome – keeping in mind that "recent" for me means within the last 30 years, especially where music is concerned – are the "Destination Wedding" and the practice at the sit-down meal of everyone in the wedding party speaking about the bride and groom with either the mandatory hyperbole of a Comintern testimonial about Stalin or the excruciating embarrassment of an idiot reminiscing about when he and the groom got drunk at a strip club. My nephew and I sat next to each other at a wedding three years ago and whenever we have texted since then one of us always says, "I think the bridesmaid is close to winding up her tearful remarks." (Some "in" jokes never get old…)

I do not know who was the first couple to say, "Hey, people, we're going to be married in Monaco, and we'd like y'all to take out a second mortgage on your home and join us." Okay, who wouldn't rather be photographed in January on the beach in Kauai than in front of a snowbank in Left Overshoe, Iowa? Then do it. But expecting your friends and relatives to up and join you just strikes me as amazingly presumptuous unless you are paying for their airline tickets and hotels. Am I wrong?

Actually, I have a niece planning a classy Destination Wedding for the young and carefree who would like to join them in Mexico but is having a nice in-country reception back in Minnesota for the geezers who can't make that. That seems a reasonable compromise.

ROAD FOOD

June 16, 2017

A few weeks ago, commenter John Pilsun suggested that he would like to see a column on interesting road food from my most recent trip from Arizona to Minnesota and back. John, your wish is my command. Column ideas are always welcome, even if it takes awhile.

I contrived to spend my first night in Van Horn, Texas, because of the quaint and delightful little hotel El Capitan, which features one of the best restaurants in the Southwest. If you haven't tasted their Pistachio-Encrusted Chicken-Fried Steak with Chipotle Gravy, you haven't lived. Key Lime Pie and the kind of waitresses who call you "Hon" and "Baby Girl."

From there, I traveled to Fort Worth, technically, Southlake, to spend two wonderful nights with my dear friend Heather, and her new fella, Bill. Frankly, if your travels take you anywhere near Texas, I would recommend a good long stay at Heather and Bill's. Not only is the price right, but Heather and Bill are both excellent cooks. She made an exquisite Beef Stew and Greek Salad in such extravagant quantity that we ate them for two meals, and Bill grilled awesome Steaks and made Breakfast Burritos to die for. Call 1-800-555-1234 for reservations. Hahaha, I kid.

Bill is not only a great guy – the best friend of the equally-great Paranoid Texan next door to us – but a true Southern Gentleman who would sooner be dragged behind wild horses than allow anyone, but especially a lady, to treat. Under extreme duress — a loaded .45 on the table — he did allow me to buy a little lunch at The Cotton Patch, a Southern-fried cooking place that correctly understands that Gravy is a beverage. I like to keep my arteries taut.

Heather and Bill packed me an emergency go-bag of Fudge from Bass Pro for the road, but that was gone at the first stop sign on the way out of their complex. I don't remember what the emergency was, but it came up awful sudden-like. With a sticky steering-wheel and an electric sugar buzz, "I persisted." My next stop was in El Dorado, Kansas, where I had a surprisingly adequate Oriental Chicken Salad with Peanuts at a little 50's-style diner.

Throughout my comedy career, I had many gigs in Des Moines and I always ate at Dudley's Cafe in Latimer, IA. They make a world-class burger and hot, crispy fries. Whatever you order, you will struggle to get the bill into double digits, so leave a huge tip. They also have a fun little gift shop with plaques that say things like: "Marriage is like a deck of cards. You start out with two hearts and a diamond and end up wanting a club and a spade."

I had planned to overnight in Ankeny, IA, and drive to Alexandria early in the morning. But I got to Ankeny and breezed right on by, rejecting motel after motel, getting ever closer to what Minnesotans simply call The Cities. This was a mistake. I hit Burnsville at 4:00 on a Thursday afternoon and 35 miles later in Maple Grove went screaming from my car into a Marriott. It was now 6:00 p.m. Yes, it had taken me two hours to go 35 miles. My patience for rush hour traffic is exceedingly low, probably because of my claustrophobia. I hate being trapped and unable to move. Mad props to those of you who have to do it every day. Twice. I know I ate in the Marriott, but do not remember what. But I do know what I drank: much.

After driving 2100 miles, on Friday the short trip "up north" to my hometown of Alexandria seemed like a little jaunt to the grocery store. I stayed six days in a hotel a few miles from Daddy's. There was a Perkins next door where my BFF, Bonnie, and I met for Girl Talk and Pie, but Perkins had taken all the joy out of it by publishing the calorie counts. What righteous scold thought THAT was a good idea? 930 calories in a piece of Peanut Butter Silk Pie? Surely you jest! That has to be computed in some sort of "dog calories."

Back to The Cities to pick Mr. AG up at the airport and begin the arduous task of clearing out personal items from 38 years of life in our Minnesota house. Sadly, we have a "mixed marriage." I like a lot of clean, open space, and Mr. AG believes that there is literally nothing that is not a precious souvenir. Think what 10,000 ATM receipts could fetch on eBay.

After five emotion-laden days of closing down our first home and celebrating our son's marriage, we packed up for home. The night before we had celebrated with our new family members in our favorite Twin Cities steakhouse – Porterhouse in Little Canada. Perfect tender steak, baked potato, and salad, just the classics done right. No silly "Reduction of Mango and Lima Bean Glaze over Salted Caramel Arugula Breading." Sometimes there is a reason why no one has ever tried a particular combination of foods before, people.

Not a lot to report, culinarily speaking, on the trip home. We just beat feet, anxious to be settled. I had been living out of a suitcase for three weeks. Good wings in Amarillo (and deep-fried cheesecake bites – why not?) with no attempt to eat the legendary "free" 6-pound steak with all the sides in an hour or less that Amarillo is famous for.

And then we were "standin' on the corner in Winslow, Arizona" ready to check into the historic La Posada Inn, with its restaurant, The Turquoise Room. Oh. My. Gawd. We started with Deep-Fried Squash Blossoms Stuffed with a Mexican cheese, and a Southwest Caesar Salad with Pumpkin Seeds. I had the Halibut on Polenta with Mushroom Broth and a bowl of gorgeous organic vegetables. Mr. AG had the Chicken grilled, over Black Beans and Roasted Corn Pudding in Endive. We both had martinis and Gelato in a Cookie Crust Cup. Beautiful presentations. A feast for all the senses. Excellent service.

The creation of Chef John Sharpe, and once rated by Conde Naste Gold List as "one of the top three restaurants in the U.S." (2009), it was easily one of the 10 best meals I've ever had in my life. And the breakfast the next morning – Orange Crepes, Turkey Sausage and Baked Eggs – was equally memorable. Google it, friends.

So that's about it, John. We drove home by 2:00 p.m. and I had half a Peanut Butter Sammich and promptly began my latest– not to be confused with, last — diet. Sigh. I think I've gained 3 lbs. just from writing this column!

RESISTING COMMON DECENCY

June 23, 2017

As I write this, Steve Scalise is in fair condition, still fighting for his life. However successful is his long road back to health and fitness (please, God), one thing is certain: he will never be the same. I know this just from my relatively minor but continuing limitations from my little rotator cuff injury more than a year ago. Which is a far cry from a bullet tearing through internal organs and shattering bone.

One of the worst conceits I've seen in my long lifetime has to be the notion that the paid masked rioters and "antifa" thugs who inspired the assassin are somehow part of a proud tradition of "Resistance." Rudeness, rampage and rioting are not "resistance."

They do all start with "R," and that is close enough for the brain-dead, lazy, chickens**t losers who have to believe themselves to be part of something important and worthy. Instead of what they actually are: just cowardly, blackshirted criminals wearing little bandana masks like they wore when they were six, playing "Cowboys and Indians." (Or Boys of Cow and Indigenous Peoples in pc language. Don't bother learning the correct language – the game is virtually illegal now on playgrounds anyway, along with Tag, Monkey Bars, Dodgeball, and chewing your bologna into the shape of a gun.)

Real resistance to massive, powerful evil has potentially dreadful real-world consequences. These spoiled brats screaming spittle-flecked obscenities at professors, wandering the campus with baseball bats, don't even get kicked out of college.

Resistance is risking torture and death in World War II Occupied France by helping to hide Jews or downed Allied pilots from the Nazis. If captured, trust me, Literally Hitler saw to it that the worst thing that happened to them was not to lose their New Year's Eve hosting gig.

Resistance is women risking torture and death in Central American dictatorships by wearing white and making a fuss about the "disappeared," who number in the thousands.

Resistance is trying to become some sort of law enforcement agent in Mexican cartel territory. Or being Coptic Christians in a Muslim country.

Resistance was smuggling matzoh into Communist Russia, or God forbid, trying to leave Russia, especially for Israel. Do you think those caught lost just their endorsement for the Squatty Potty? No. They lost everything – housing, jobs, families. "Wintering" in Siberia. Or lifelong confinement in a "mental hospital."

And Resistance was the Reverend Doctor Martin Luther King marching for the most elemental human rights and dignity and risking beatings, jail and death threats that were eventually carried out. The pusillanimous morons protesting white women selling burritos or demanding that all white professors exile themselves from a campus are not only NOT part of his legacy; they are simply crude and ugly racists themselves.

Even apart from the violence and obscenity of their behavior, Dr. King would have had nothing to do with them. They are not "reverse" racists, a phrase coined a few decades ago; they are just regular old garden-variety racists and loud-n'-proud bigots, plain and simple. As vile as any hooded coward. If you hate someone because of the color of his/her skin, then you are a racist no matter what the color of yours. Own it.

I understand the shall-remain-nameless wretch with the severed head has been done to death by now. I want to address her apologists – lookin' at YOU, Al Franken – who are trying to pass off a Presidential beheading in effigy as just a First Amendment statement, a little prank gone awry. These are people who have lost all connection with human decency.

Even to describe the image as a "joke" is an affront to every comedian living and dead. What is funny in any context about a beheading? It is a vile and unspeakable act carried out by savages. There is no way that anyone who hates Trump could despise him any more than I despised the entire last Administration down to the last overpaid porn-surfing time-server. And I would have been exactly as appalled at such an image of Obama or Holder or Lois Lerner. Hell, I was angry when Obama was treated rudely in Russia: hey, you jerks, that's MY President, even though I didn't vote for him. Shake his damn hand or don't invite him there. In a civil society, manners should still count for something. (I guess Obama hadn't yet attained the maximum "flexibility" he promised Russia's Medvedev. Who knows? Maybe he did a lot of yoga when he wasn't golfing.)

Al Franken said the decapitated bloody head image was a "mistake." Really? That is a definition of "mistake" with which I am not familiar. The empty-headed twit had to obtain the Trump head; she had to cover it in fake blood; she had to plan for a photo shoot and pay the photographer. She had to have makeup and hair done. What part of all that deliberate action was a "mistake"? If that is not a perfect definition of premeditation, then I don't know what is.

A "mistake" is what I did the other day: I put nine eggs on to boil for my famous Deviled Eggs for Poker Night and went away to write a column. I failed to set the timer to 15 minutes and got carried away writing (Yeah, hard to believe, I know). The water boiled dry, the eggs exploded all over my kitchen, and I thought at first they were gunshots. I grabbed my Walther PPQ and screamed out to find out if my dear Mr. AG was alright. Now THAT is a "mistake." Or possibly, not-all-that-early Alzheimer's, but definitely not a deliberate act.

Thank God there were no killer eggs in big enough pieces to have to shoot them. My kitchen is a very richochet-rich environment with lots of granite.

MY FIRST ELECTION

June 30, 2017

A study has confirmed what everybody already suspected: in 2008 some 5.7 MILLION non-citizens voted. I do not know if that also includes the dead, the felonious, and the enthusiastic voters who voted many times. Can't happen; racist to suggest it does, says The Left.

Bovine excrement, says Ammo Grrrll. Mine eyes have seen the glory. The year was 1964 and I had just turned 18 a month earlier. I was a freshman in college at Northwestern University, in Evanston, Illinois. I was a Goldwater Girl. The voting age was still 21, so I was not even eligible to vote, but I was keenly interested in the election.

The Republicans were looking for volunteers to be Poll-Watchers, preferably volunteers from way out of town who were not aware of the places we were about to be sent in Chicago.

It would have been difficult to find anyone more sheltered than I was that Fall, anyone more likely to have just fallen off the turnip truck. And so my new boyfriend – the only one before Mr. AG — who would not even turn 18 until late December, and I signed up to be Poll-Watchers on the South Side of Chicago, at 63rd and Cottage Grove. Seriously.

As we rode from Evanston south on the El at 5 a.m., we held hands and felt like we were important little cogs in the democratic process. At some point the two little old ladies with net shopping bags who had been sitting across from us yakking in Polish got off the El. We did not yet realize that ours were now the only white faces we would see for the next 18 hours. And we still had several more stops to go before our destination. This did not really disturb us, mainly because we were too naive to be worried.

We arrived about 6:30 and went into the polling place and introduced ourselves with some sort of letter from the state Republicans. The Democrats were already there and, not surprisingly, were all black. In fact, two of them had just volunteered to be the "Republican" poll-watchers. They seemed frankly astonished to see two little white teenagers.

We sat at our own little table with tablets to "observe" and take notes on any "irregularities." The irregularities began right out of the box as our first voter got his paper ballot, went into the voting booth and emerged almost immediately feeling "sick," and quickly running off.

We had been alerted to this. We were told that the ward heelers were paying for votes. But how to guarantee that your bribed voters actually voted "right"? I mean, you can't eliminate sheer stupidity. Remember the "butterfly" ballot in Florida? Here's the solution: Just have the first guy pocket and bring out a BLANK ballot. Then the Precinct Captain marks the ballot himself and gives it to the next guy in line, who puts it in his pocket, gets a blank one from the person handing them out, puts the pre-marked one in the ballot box and returns the pocketed blank one to the Captain to be marked again. It was called "chain" balloting. Clever!

My boyfriend went outside to look at the line and saw the Precinct Captain openly handing out dollar bills. Later when they ran out of dollar bills, they were handing out pounds of bacon out of a cooler. This went on all day long.

We were writing furiously. Eventually, the polls closed and it was time to count the ballots. At this point, an imposing woman came over and told us we could leave now. She said that because we were not 21, we were actually not eligible to be poll-watchers at all, especially during the counting. (Well done, Republicans!) She said they could have got rid of us earlier, but agreed to let us stay until the counting since we had come such a long way.

We didn't argue. Back in the day, teenagers didn't argue with adults, let alone scream obscenities at them. It was now pitch black out and two long city blocks back to the El stop.

When we got back to campus, I ran into a tough Italian Chicago native who was in my Advanced French class. He was an older student, a Social Work major and part-time youth worker working with gangs on the South Side. He said we were lucky to be alive. First of all, we had no money and absolutely nothing worth stealing, and secondly, perhaps the Lord dispatches special angels to guard the terminally stupid.

Goldwater, of course, would experience a decisive, yea, crushing defeat, winning the electoral votes of just five Southern states, plus Arizona. It made me wonder why the Democrats had bothered to squander money on votes. But who knows how many votes were not only paid for but counted multiple times in Chicago, in Detroit, in East St. Louis, in Milwaukee?

In the most recent special election that Ms. Handel won, uh, "handily," the losing losers cried losingly that there was "voter suppression" by such racist events as A Rainy Night in Georgia. Evidently only Democrats are afraid to get wet. Sad. Here's a new entitlement: mandatory umbrellas on Election Day! (Yeah, I know; don't give them any ideas!)

The problem with dead people and non-citizens voting, with people going from polling place to polling place doing "same-day" registration in Minnesota, is not simply that it absolutely perverts one man-one vote democracy. But if 300 ineligible voters cast ballots for Al Franken, say – felons, non-citizens, the deceased – obviously that means the other side needs 300 legitimate ballots just to pull the counter back to zero. It is outrageously unfair.

From that November day in 1964 to the present, I have never really had much confidence in the integrity of the electoral process. And I will never, ever believe the bald-faced lie that there is little or no cheating in elections. I have seen it with my own eyes and no race-baiting demagogue will ever convince me otherwise. There is one reason and one reason alone not to clean up the voter rolls and not to have to show picture ID to vote and that is to enable cheating. Period. That the citizens of my former home state voted the Picture ID measure down in flames is just one more yuge reason I am glad to call Arizona home.

JULY, AUGUST, SEPTEMBER

The blistering hot summer in Arizona should provide a Get Out of Writing Free card, citing Baked Brain Syndrome. No, really, it's a thing. How else to explain California? Haha. I kid California. Which is known for its robust sense of humor.

So, the heat may not excuse less-than-stellar writing, but it did provide the impetus for the first summer ever to get the heck out of town and go to the mountains of beautiful Prescott, Arizona. Which also provided the grist for the first column of the second Ammo Grrrll Quarter – about our very first ever rodeo.

From there, I write about Mr. AG's parsing of the difference between vitamins for "Adults" and vitamins for "Men". A discussion ensues of whether or not Men are actually Adults. Your mileage may vary. Next up is the news that you COULD have bid in an auction to win the tear-stained dress that Lena Dunham wore the night of the 2016 election. It's too late now, of course, and you may not be a Size 18 anyway, but it did provide fodder for a pretty funny column. Next up is a description of a microaggression in a hotel followed by a discussion of "punching down", the novel idea that certain people are not ever entitled to fight back.

I must have been on a roll thinking about privilege in general because the very next week there is a "quiz" to determine just how privileged YOU are. During the next week, I returned briefly from Prescott to the Dusty Little Village down in the hot valley and noticed a sign proclaiming that the roadside vendors for kettle corn, shrimp, oranges, mattresses, art, and the like were now taking credit cards. We columnists take our topics where we find them, and with great gratitude.

As summer bakes its way to slightly-cooler Autumn, we visit the propensity of the Perpetually Enraged Left to tear down statues, burn books and generally try to erase any American or World History it deems offensive. Which is pretty much all of it. We end the quarter with The Great Racist Banana Peel Debacle, then bumper stickers identifying the driver as a member of The Resistance, and perpetual complaints that The Rich aren't paying enough taxes by people who have never paid enough taxes to fund a dozen eggs' worth of Food Stamps. Finally, Nancy Pelosi mangles her metaphors, and October is upon us.

NOT MY FIRST RODEO

July 7, 2017

Oh, wait! It WAS! Mr. AG and I recently visited Prescott, AZ, where it is about 15-20 degrees cooler, on average, than back in the Dusty Little Village. Prescott hosts The World's Oldest Rodeo every summer and we bought tickets to one of the nights. Mr. AG thought we should go two nights in a row, so the second night we could finally say, "This is not my first rodeo," and be telling the truth.

Anyway, I loved it. And what's not to love? Pageantry, patriotism, and pathetically-unhealthy snacks! Plus prayer. The entire Clinger trifecta. We were experiencing a dangerous wildfire in the very near vicinity and the whole crowd bowed to pray for the firefighters.

Rodeo is clearly a family event. There were hordes of young children there, sporting hats and boots and one adorable little fellow, maybe three years old, holding Daddy's hand and wearing a t-shirt that said, "Not my first rodeo."

There were many stands and booths with clothing on offer sporting such sentiments as "Cowgirls don't cry. They reload." The parking lot was a Sea of Silverados with nary an "I'm With HER" bumper sticker in sight. Which certainly set it apart from the Minneapolis airport or even the Trader Joe's across the street from our hotel.

Now I love Trader Joe's. They stood firm against the BDS Jew-hating slimebuckets picketing Trader Joe's for the crime of selling Israeli feta cheese. God Bless 'Em. (I buy a pound

a week to support Israel and need a second Feta Fridge…)
But the parking lot is a hilarious tribute to Virtue Signaling: "I
am a vegetarian and I vote." "I'm already against the next
war." "Love Trumps Hate." And so forth. When I shop there, I
delight in wearing my C2 Tactical shirt with the crossed
pistols and skull on the back. Nothing says "feminine" to me
like a skull, although on the shirt, the skull is atop a bed of
roses, which I think makes all the difference.

Meanwhile, back to the rodeo. I was somewhat surprised –
though I shouldn't have been – to note that the great majority
of the rodeo contestants in all the events were on the smaller
side. They tended to be slender, ridiculously athletic, and
looked strong as hell. All of which would serve them well
when roping steers, jumping on and off horses, and trying to
stay on a bucking bronco or Raging Bull. There was a
certain swagger to the stars, a kind of vibrant "toxic
masculinity" so hated by the leftists' womyns. Toxic
masculinity is my very favorite kind of masculinity, if only
because it annoys the feminists so much.

The incredibly interesting and informative rodeo program
explained that most rodeo events flowed naturally from the
jobs cowboys did every day. Bull riding being the glaring
exception and so exciting that it is saved for the closing act.
My late Uncle George was a veterinarian in South Dakota
who was gored three times in his career. He had a lot of
respect for bulls.

You do have to wonder about the mental state of the first
guy who decided, "What the hell, I think I'm gonna just get
on this dangerous thousand-pound animal with horns, spur
him in the side, put one hand in the air, and see what
happens." No contestant clung to the bull for dear life with
his second hand, which I thought would be a tough instinct to
overcome, and not a single rider screamed, "For God's
Sake, someone HELP ME!" when the gate opened. I

became the Designated Screamer for the event, so soon we had plenty of room around us in the crowded bleachers.

Anybody who pretends to believe that males do not have some risk-taking gene absent in most females has never watched little boys at play. There's a reason, besides lack of opportunity, that two bicycle shop ladies named Orvilla and Wilhelmina Wright didn't become the first to fly. Not that Amelia Earhart was a slouch, wherever she may be. Plenty of skill and guts, but evidently with my unfortunate sense of direction. (I always liked to think she was just on a Caribbean island somewhere, living it up with a new boyfriend.)

Both the audience and the stars of the rodeo were a nice multi-culti mix, which, despite the reflexive slanders about us, is very natural here in Deplorable-Land. Not so many African-Americans, but plenty of Native Americans and Mexicans.

One of the most heavily-cheered acts was a gentleman named Tomas Garcilazo, whose family for many generations has learned the skill of "La Charreria." It is a combination of rope artistry and horseback riding which culminates in his standing up on the saddle doing impossible things with a 30 foot rope while his beautiful horse stands stock still. The program listed among his credits that he had performed at Disney's Wild West Show in Paris, France, and the Buffalo Bill Wild West Show touring Europe. Not even to mention the White House. Maybe Bill and Hillary rented out the Lincoln Bedroom to his horse; the program wasn't specific.

One of my favorite events was the Ladies' Barrel Racing. Fit, fast, and beautifully-costumed ladies ride like the wind around 3 barrels and then on the straightaway in a rigorously-timed event. Last year's World Champion, Mary Burger, has career earnings over $600,000. Go, Mary! And I bet that doesn't count endorsement money. I hear there's a job opening for a spokesgal for the Squatty Potty.

There was a veteran emcee whose job it was to fill dead air every second. He told a funny joke which I will include here for free. He used his colleagues in the joke, and so will I.

John, Paul and Scott are (God Forbid!) in an unfortunate accident and go to Heaven. They are surprised to learn that in Heaven they will be assigned new wives. John's new wife is shockingly unattractive and he asks why. "Well," says St. Peter, "once you cheated on your taxes." Paul steps up and his new wife makes John's look like Marilyn Monroe. Turns out one time he also cheated on his taxes. Scott is thrilled to find he has been assigned a beautiful, shapely blonde! When he asks St. Peter how he got so lucky, Pete says, "She cheated on her taxes."

I'M A MAN!

July 14, 2017

Mr. AG and I take a multi-vitamin every day. Never one to miss a marketing opportunity, Centrum makes more or less-identical vitamins labeled "Women," "Men," and the one I take for Geezer-Americans labeled Adults Fifty-Plus called Centrum Silver. As I was shaking my vitamin out of the bottle, offering one to Mr. AG, he said something both hilarious and with a kernel of truth: "No, not that one. I'm not an 'Adult'; I'm a 'Man'!"

I learned that it IS possible to pass Cheerios through your nose! Even with blueberries.

Now, beloved gentlemen fans of my writing, I defy you to find a single anti-male sentence in any of my columns. There are over 160 of them in the Archives. We'll wait…

I love and adore men, specifically the ones in my life – husband, son, step-grandson, nephews, brother, dear friends, my Papa – but even generally, I think the male sex is one of two equally splendid and complementary ones. But, as Larry the Cable Guy would say, "Come ON, THAT'S funny, I don't care who you are!"

And I think that there is something wonderfully "non-adult" about a lot of men's activities. In fact, I think one of the reasons that women are sometimes critical of these activities is that they are jealous of the irrationally exuberant fun men have.

So what men's activities do I think are less than adult? Well, very few women will go topless in groups to sporting events in freezing weather with their faces painted in team colors and supportive messages spelled out collectively on their chests. Though this would not be unwelcome in many circles. And it would certainly bring beloved Cubs sports announcer Harry Carey back from the dead to comment appreciatively. Harry and his cameraman could find scantily clad female fans in the bleachers like heat-seeking missiles. Harry loved summer.

You will find very few women making up pretend sports teams and obsessively checking their cellphones during a nice Golden Anniversary dinner to see if their Pretend Pitcher blew a Save or their Pretend Second Baseman has an oblique injury and is on the DL.

In the Fantasy League that Mr. AG and our son have belonged to for a couple of decades, there is one owner team made up of two women, one of whom is actually a sitting judge in the state of Minnesota, which should give you pause. But these highly intelligent women choose their players based strictly on who has – dare I say it in a family blog? – cute butts! Oh, for "sexist"! If they run for office, weepy traumatized men will have to knit pink "butt hats" to protest. Their Fantasy League record is not wonderful, but they really have fun screening and assessing prospective players for their team.

Not to brag, but we actually do count as a friend a REAL owner of an ACTUAL major league baseball team! Mike, should you decide to emphasize guys with cute butts in assembling your roster next year in order to attract more lady fans, possibly including your wife, I would selflessly offer to help select them. Haha. I kid, of course. Kidding is what I do. (But, seriously, call me.)

I also love the fiercely competitive streak in almost all men. An orthopaedic surgeon told a friend of mine that he could make a living solely on cutthroat family picnic volleyball games. For forty years now the people who would lose every fair competition have tried to drive that streak into oblivion: the participation trophies, the failure to keep score in Little League or soccer, the emphasis on "group" projects and "cooperation" rather than individual effort and competition, banning valedictorians, colleges with no grades. The dreary list goes on and on.

Oh, don't get me wrong. Cooperation in many circumstances is a great and necessary thing. (CNN news crawl: "H8TR Ammo Grrrll Against Cooperation!"): bucket brigades, quilting bees, research projects, surgery theaters. But in almost every group project I have been involved in there have been the doers and the slackers. When I had a partner in Biology, I was definitely the slacker, gagging at the smell of formaldehyde and none too thrilled with the innards of a frog either. Thank you, Judy, for getting me through! We were "partners" and she did all the work. We both got an "A."

Anyway, one of my most vivid experiences with men's competitive nature involved lawyers. (There's a surprise!) Many years ago, in a galaxy far far away, Mr. AG was an associate in a very big deal law firm in the Twin Cities. This law firm organized a Retreat to try to get their guys and gals to relax for a weekend. In order to drag them away from their offices – this was so long ago that everyone wasn't yet permanently connected to a virtual office via electronics – they had to shanghai them to a resort hundreds of miles north of the Twin Cities lest they sneak back down overnight and work.

But in order that they not implode from toxic testosterone buildup (even the women) or pent-up adrenaline, they organized a whole series of athletic competitions –

volleyball, golf, of course, and softball. And what happened? It rained, Noah-style, for two solid days. The water in the parking lot was up to my knees, although that isn't saying a lot. And – on their own – the fellas organized a killer afternoon of what I called MMA Full-Contact Charades. It's a miracle no one died. I've never had more fun in my life. Lacking entirely in the normal fear of looking like an idiot, I happen to be a whiz at Charades.

A VERY MINOR CELEBRITY'S AUCTION

July 21, 2017

I recently read a first-person account by a woman who had been a "proud lesbian" until her partner up and decided she was actually a man. This woman expected to be a Professional Gay Woman for life with all the dual rights and privileges to which she was entitled, and suddenly she finds herself married to a regular old garden-variety MAN like the rest of us non-special heterosexual women.

Not only that, but since it's verboten to suggest that the transgender person hadn't ALWAYS been a man, this woman had been with a man all along, thus jeopardizing her status as a lesbian, proud or not. That's gotta rock your world. On top of that, her partner CHOSE Toxic Masculinity! She was born a Fabulous Female, but OPTED to join Team Terrible, The No Good Very Bad Oppressor Gender. What the heck? Somebody is lying here: either men are not as hideous as advertised, or a woman who freely chooses to become one is not a "transgender" but a gender traitor, deliberately inflicting another icky man on the world!

To the woman's credit, I guess, she tells us that this man is still the same dear partner he had always been and she is going to stay with him. Whatever. Wait for the other shoe to drop – when he can't stand being hectored for contributing to Rape Culture and causing all the world's ills any more and announces that he is a GAY man and dumps her for another guy.

Sorry. But if Mr. AG declares one day that he is a lady – exactly the same chance as the UN apologizing for its nauseating anti-Semitism before disbanding in abject shame – we could still be good friends and I would give him my Brisket recipe and pie crust secrets. Possibly, we could go shoe-shopping together for Size 13 high heels, so he could be a 6'7" woman.

But no, we would not continue to be married. That's how narrow-minded I am. I'm pretty sure he feels even stronger about the chances he would stay married to a 5 foot tall high-strung tiny man with a crewcut and the mandatory silly facial hair. I mean, I might give it a go if I thought it would help me have a better sense of direction. Or ANY sense of direction.

But that's not actually what this column is about. It's about a whole different forehead-slapper and a wonderful romp down Memory Lane. Lena Dunham, who might have gone as long as a week without making a fool of herself for publicity, has announced that she is auctioning off the very dress in which she cried on election night! Oh Em Gee, you guys. Who wouldn't want in on THAT action?

Yes, her candidate LOST and the other one won! Something that has never happened before in the history of The Republic! (Well, ten times to ME, but who's counting?) It is totally unacceptable that virtually all of Hollywood – the Beautiful People, the Smart People, the Rich People Whose Important Job Is Pretending to be Someone Else – wanted the OTHER candidate to win and yet she did not! And in this new Dystopia where women are going to be living out *"The Handmaid's Tale"* with forced breeding, naturally, Lachrymose Lena is going to donate the proceeds of this auction to Planned Parenthood.

The EGO on this woman-child! What would anyone want with or do with her tear-stained dress? Do you put it in one of those vacuum-sealed plastic bags for posterity: "This dress once belonged to a mediocre actress who lived to prance around nekkid. Am I lucky, or what, to have this?" Has the garment been laundered since November 8th, or would it fetch a bigger price if it weren't – like sweaty "game-worn" sports jerseys?

These are certainly questions for the ages. But it did open up some fundraising possibilities for me. As a semi-anonymous "celebrity" with tens of fans of my column, I am auctioning off a (M) T-shirt with pictures of many calibers of cartridges. The shirt, which I got at a gun show, sports the slogan, "America… learning the metric system one millimeter at a time." I was wearing it the night of the election when I stayed up til dawn in stunned disbelief and Irish Coffee-fueled exuberance. It is clean and ready to wear upon arrival.

I will throw in the warm Walmart slippers (S) with the slip-proof feet in which I jumped up and down doing the Happy Dance in unbridled joy when each Rust Belt state went to Trump and it became clear that Hillary Clinton would NEVER be President of the United States.

Act before midnight, and I will include the cheap adjustable ring from the finger with which I have repeatedly pressed "Play" to watch the YouTube meltdowns of the unbiased neutral media. Oh, the long, sad faces when "their" candidate lost Wisconsin, Michigan, Iowa, Ohio, North Carolina, Pennsylvania, and Florida! I have watched my candidate lose on most election nights – and yet, the next day, I still called the winner "my President" — but I have never seen the media root more openly for one side without a fig leaf of objectivity.

Watching Rachel Maddow's distressed little face come perilously close to losing her trademark snotty smirk as she informed her stunned fan base that "No, you haven't died and gone to hell. This is your life now," was one of the highlights of my life. But I don't get out much. Just hours earlier, she had animatedly assured that base that even IF Donald won all the toss-ups and even one electoral vote in Maine, he would still lose. Oopsie!

At first I watched these YouTube freak-outs several times a day, as much to convince myself that it had really happened as to gloat. Okay, mostly to gloat. I am down to every couple of weeks now, whenever I need a lift. It never gets old, does it? In my opinion, America had one last chance to pull back from the abyss and her patriots took it! Justice Gorsuch alone was worth it, no matter what else happens going forward.

All profits from the auction will be divided between Project Veritas and my personal charity, The Ammo Grrrll Wildlife Fund. Remember, if you don't give, I can't lead a Wild Life. Let the bidding begin.

MICROAGRESSION IN ABILENE

July 28, 2017

This happened to me on my Spring road trip from the Dusty Little Village to my hometown in Minnesota. Naturally, I have been in therapy ever since. First, to recover, and second, to try to establish enough of a case for emotional distress that I can sue. Then I plan to write a book and possibly design a line of t-shirts that I can peddle. (Late, Late Middle Aged Lives Matter!) I am hoping that Gal Gadot will play me in the obligatory movie – No Hotel Chain for Old Ladies — in the unlikely event that Scarlett Johansson is unavailable.

I can't count the number of times strangers have asked me, "Aren't you that pert girl, Scarlett?" Or possibly, "Isn't that shirt from Carhartt?" My hearing isn't what it used to be.

So, what happened? Trigger warning! Get your Play-Doh!

I had driven from Van Horn, TX to Abilene, on my way to Fort Worth to stay with the friends, Heather and Bill, I referenced in my Road Food column. I am pretty sure Abilene is not part of the always-windy Panhandle. But it should have some sort of honorary status as a windy gol-darn place. The reason I didn't go all the way to Ft. Worth, was that I was not due there until the next day and didn't want to just show up saying, "Hey, I know you thought I was coming tomorrow, but this is your lucky day, cuz here I am already! What's for brunch?"

Heather and Bill would have been perfectly gracious when I knocked on their door and, eventually, probably answered. But, you know, there are limits, even to a 57-year friendship. And I know for certain that Heather owns a .357 magnum and has quite a startle reflex.

I don't actually want to mention the name of the hotel in which this travesty occurred, because – unlike leftists – I don't want anyone to lose his or her or xer job. I love people to have jobs.

I had arrived at the hotel way too early for normal check-in. However, noticing that I was a Gold Frequent Stayer with 50 nights at the chain, the front desk clerk gave me my key and promised my room would be cleaned next. I was welcome to hang out in the lobby. I thanked her and decided to spend the time walking briskly about the property. I try to walk a minimum of an hour a day. I first tried walking around outside. The gale-force winds blew me back inside in one pass around the parking lot. Plus it had started raining. My Mama always spoke disparagingly of people who "didn't know enough to come in out of the rain."

The hotel had a little meeting room and convention center wing attached to it. I walked the halls there. Sadly, the wind had rearranged my long pony tail into a style I call "Escaped Mental Patient." It is possible this hairdo, combined with old jeans, Ruger shirt, and Day-Glo Aqua running shoes (on sale on Amazon because apparently no sane person wanted that color…), gave me a somewhat alarming appearance and set in motion a "Mauve" Alert. (Crazy Old Lady, Possibly Homeless except for the $300 Maui Jim shades, a birthday gift.)

The walking itself could have raised the alert from "Mauve" to "Puce". Almost nobody in America walks any more; Walmart is filled with people in motorized carts who are simply too fat to walk. People drive half a block to our mailboxes in the DLV even when it isn't summer.

In any event, after walking for about 30 minutes, I saw a

woman from Housekeeping who had been stacking towels in a closet in the convention area, and eyeing me suspiciously, decide that enough was enough. She sprinted to the lobby and shortly thereafter, a different front desk person, a man this time, approached me and asked me – none too politely and in front of other people – if I were a registered guest.

Gifted with a dominant "Smart-Assery" Gene from birth, I almost said, "No, I live in Arizona, but I have driven 859 miles just to walk in your fine lobby." Instead, I just politely pulled my little key card out of my jeans pocket, and said, "Of course I am. Why do you ask?" There was no apology or any explanation for their concern.

Here's the thing: every single person involved was African-American. The first woman clerk, the skittish maid, and the gentleman who approached me.

Let us imagine for one moment what would have happened if it had been the other way around. Suppose an all-white staff had approached a small, elderly black woman walking around and asked her if she really belonged there? As Rush would say, "Katie, bar the door!"

What possible other reason could there have been for her to be queried, but raaacism? The Rev'rund Jessuh Jackson would have been there on the next flight out from whatever camera he was in front of to Abilene. CNN would have blamed Trump (#IsMyPresident) for the racist atmosphere that would have allowed such a humiliating incident to have occurred. The woman would have had free nights in perpetuity at the hotel chain (plus a scholarship to Duke University) and nobody would have been satisfied until every employee involved had lost his or her job and mandatory Diversity Training inflicted upon those who remained.

The next morning I was walking down the hall from my room

to the elevator. Two maids were talking loudly, one of whom had alerted the front desk clerk to check me out. She was facing away from me, peppering her language with many "f-words" and even the "m-f-word" as her colleague tried in vain to signal her to shush. As I walked past she looked pretty startled. What if I said something to a manager about her inappropriate language? You know how us clingy Deplorables are always trying to force our morals down others' throats.

Once again, I resisted the temptation to say, "And, Top o' the Effin' Mornin' to YOU, too." I smiled, wished God's blessings upon them both, and sat in the breakfast area making notes for this future column.

PUNCHING DOWN

August 4, 2017

A co-worker of mine from long ago stood 6'4" and weighed in at about 240 pounds of mostly muscle. He said that in his late teens and early twenties he and his buddies would often ride around to bars in neighboring suburbs and small towns looking for a fight. It was the '50s, no weapons were involved, and the fight usually ended with the first bloody nose or split lip. Just bored young men with a lot of testosterone, phony ID, and not a lot to do.

He said he won all but a couple of fights, largely because he was too stubborn to fall down, and he quit the pointless exercise when he got engaged. But he told me something that stuck with me. He said the worst guy to fight was somebody considerably smaller than he was. He called this "The No-Win Situation." He said, "If I cleaned the guy's clock, the whole bar would turn on me for picking on a little guy, even if he was drunk, obnoxious and clearly started it. And if he ambushed me and knocked me around a bit before I got in a punch, the crowd would still cheer for him as the underdog wailin' on the big guy. I could not win."

Apparently, while I wasn't paying attention, this No-Win Situation got formalized into a prohibition against "punching down." A strict pecking order got established that I did not get to vote on and anybody who takes on someone from a lower rung of that order – physically, certainly, but even verbally or ideologically – is guilty of punching down. What a load of crap!

In practice, what this means is that a gossip-mongering,

nasty dingbat with double-digit SAT scores, a leaky facelift and a silly, flirty publicity picture can say anything she wants about anyone, including the President of the United States. She has a job solely because of nepotism, and a Great Big Daily Megaphone. But if the President says anything snarky back, he is punching down, sexist, undignified, impeachable.

I strongly disagree. And as a small, late-late-middle aged female with a bum shoulder, I should come under the umbrella of punching down protection as much as anyone who isn't also gay, Muslim, black, transgender or illegal.

For many years, it was considered high humor in movies for a woman to slap a man in the face, sucker-punch him, or kick him in the crotch. These were not women who were either superheroes, or in any way abused in the plots, who were bravely defending themselves. These were just ordinary women who were mad at the men in their lives and felt they could slap, punch and kick without consequence. I could give dozens of examples. It was probably so common, almost obligatory, for a time there that you didn't even notice it.

Not only was this spectacularly unfunny and predictable, it also gave a dangerous and misleading impression to women of what could happen next in the real world.

After some thoroughly nauseating examples of domestic violence caught on video, there have been several campaigns saying, "Never hit women." Never, never, never. Okay. Fair dinkum. Who could disagree? But why aren't women also told never to hit men? Not only because they will lose in the end if it all goes south, but because it is just as wrong even though they probably cannot hurt a man quite as badly. That darned testosterone advantage!

When I lived in San Francisco, even with our massive white

privilege we had no car and I took the trolley everywhere I went. On one particular line I took to work there was a wacky middle-aged woman who was a frequent passenger. She would come up to random strangers and yank their hair, yelling, "I pull hair!" Not encountering any resistance, she later escalated to punching. (A lesson, that…)

I was 25 years old and 8 months pregnant when she decided it was my turn. I had gotten to my feet – itself no small accomplishment — preparing to get off the trolley when she got in my face and punched me in the belly, saying her usual "I punch people!" mantra. I had lost two babies before this pregnancy and I was in no mood to take a punch to the stomach. I hit her square in the chest with the heel of my hand and knocked her into, and almost over, an empty seat, saying, "Well, I punch BACK, you (bad word) lunatic!" In truth, so terrified was I for my baby, I wanted to keep punching, but I just hit her the once.

I wish we had had picture-taking cellphones back then because the look on her face was priceless. Yes, she was probably "crazy" – as though that automatically excuses all rotten behavior — but not so irrational that she was incapable of absorbing a lesson. She was totally shocked that anyone fought back. I cannot certify that she stopped this behavior for good, but whenever she saw me, she moved as fast and as far away from me as she could get. And she never hit another person again in my presence.

Clearly, in general, we do not hit back children, the mentally-challenged, the elderly, even if they hit us first. (These are, in fact, some of the targets for the odious "Knock-out Game" popularized in the Obama era and given scant attention in the media because the wrong people were doing the punching.) Civilized people didn't need to be lectured not to do this. Probably 99 percent of American men have never hit a female in their lives, if you don't count sisters. But the notion that you can't criticize women, after fifty years of feminism yapping about how equal (or superior) women are in all things is ludicrous and embarrassing.

Take Maxine Waters and Nancy Pelosi– PULEEZE. Sorry, Henny. These awful women are in very powerful positions and at least one is a billionaire. To declare a "no-go" zone from pointing out that one has a Carter-era speed limit IQ and the other would be a good poster girl for dementia may seem merciful, gallant, even. But that mercy is misplaced. They should not be exempted from criticism just for being stupid, female and/or black. They punch viciously and continuously, expecting, like the woman on the trolley, like the women in those movies, to get a perpetual free pass. They have designer handbags stuffed with Race Cards and Sex Cards to play whenever anyone does fight back. There are no expiration dates on these prized cards ever.

Here's what I believe with all my heart: There is no such thing as punching "down." A punch is a punch and if you punch me first, there is a very good chance you will be punched back. As comedian Ron White would say, "I've seen me do it."

HOW PRIVILEGED ARE YOU?

August 11, 2017

Let me stipulate right out of the box that I consider myself blessed beyond any possible sense of merit. Blessed by being raised by two stable, loving parents in a great small town in the Midwest; blessed by finding a wonderful spouse early in life; blessed with good health for myself and loved ones. I thank The Holy One, Blessed be He, for these blessings every day, multiple times.

But "privilege" per se? It is a stupid word in most of the contexts in which the "intersectional" mush-minds use it. Mostly it is used as a bludgeon with which to browbeat anyone who has worked hard and achieved anything. And also to excuse massive laziness and the eagerness to demand benefits unearned except on the basis of some accident of birth, like color or gender.

The whole school of thought makes me sick – not just for the inherent unfairness of blaming people for reading to their children, for being smarter than the average bear, for "not building" the many businesses they worked 12 hour days to sustain. But even more for the disaster that professional victimhood inflicts upon those who rely on it to skate through life.

Let us look in the harsh light of day upon a few choice examples of people who fit into the category of multiply oppressed. Let us look at a person who is black and also a woman. How about Ms. Halle Berry. By Intersectional Victimhood Theory, Ms. Berry should be almost too oppressed to speak. Perhaps being so physically beautiful that she was once voted "the 6th most beautiful woman in the WORLD" eased some of the pain and opened a couple of doors for her. Her net worth in 2012 was estimated at $70 million. Oh, and she was also an honor student in her high school, so there's a demerit for being "cognitively privileged."

Though I am loaded with White Privilege – my kin are just paleskins back to the beginning of time with nary a 1/32 Pretend Cherokee to make higher cheekbones — for some reason nobody is interested in casting me as a Bond Girl emerging like a vision from the sea in a bikini. God knows, I wouldn't pay to see that. So it would seem that even White Privilege is trumped by Beauty Privilege. Not even to mention Youth Privilege. There was a time 50 years ago when the bikini part would not even have been that far-fetched, but alas, the airbrushing required in late, late middle age would have used up so much of the budget that Bond would have had to buy his tux at Ross (Dress for Less).

Mr. Stephen Hawking is not only a man, and a white man, but he also has "cognitive privilege" up the wazoo. But what able-bodied Hispanic gay woman would like to trade places with him? Volunteers? Step right up. Maybe things are a tad more complicated than would appear at first blush. Even profoundly disabled, Mr. Hawking has a net worth of $20 million.

Neither do I enjoy Height Privilege. Not only will I never play professional basketball, but I have to risk life and limb standing on 2-step stools and kitchen chairs in order to reach even the middle shelves above my counters. My old performing contract used to stipulate that I needed a 2-foot riser, if the room didn't have a stage. I am almost exactly the same size standing at floor level as most people are sitting in a folding chair and no one past the first two rows could see me. Sad.

Somehow, despite being born black, Michael Jordan, awash in Height Privilege and Talent Privilege, and Work Ethic Privilege, has managed to accumulate a net worth of $1.3 BILLION. There are about 50,000 coal miners in the U.S., 3% of whom are black, and a tiny handful of whom are women. One site I looked at on American net worth said the average net worth for someone 45-54 years old, excluding equity in a home, was about $25,000. Though coal mining actually pays pretty well, it is not inconceivable that Michael Jordan has a net worth equivalent to all the white, male coal miners in the United States – COMBINED.

So stick your "Intersectionality" in your hat. And we haven't even got to Oprah yet.

Ellen DeGeneres, gay woman, very high on the Victimhood Scale — though I've never known her to play that card — has a net worth of $200 Million. Not only would she never have to work another day in her life, but with even a modest interest rate, she should be able to live off just the INTEREST on that forever even with a Hollywood lifestyle. And a regular person could live off the interest on the interest! Well done, Ellen!

I'm sure if you are able to stay awake long enough to plow through the academic gibberish that is the Intersectional Theory, there will be some kind of codicil in there saying that "sure, there are exceptions." But my guess is that the reason for those exceptions is never explained honestly. How could it be? It would negate the whole theory if the answer were as simple as talent, hard work, attitude, grit, making responsible decisions about drugs and criminality and sex, and then a little blind, dumb luck.

Maybe someone has very little talent. But hard work, attitude, grit and responsibility are available to any person in this great and good land of opportunity.

My Daddy – not remotely a Participation Trophy kind of guy – always used to tell me, "People who are good at excuses are seldom good at anything else." Intersectional Theory is just one big excuse with a faux intellectual veneer. Which is soooo much easier than actually putting in the work. Remember Rosie Ruiz, the woman who slid into the 1980 Boston Marathon in the last half mile or so? She didn't train at 4:00 a.m.; she didn't sweat; she didn't battle shin splints or calluses. She just budged the line and tried to carry off the trophy. Is there any better definition of Affirmative Action?

FINANCING KETTLE CORN

August 18, 2017

Sometimes, when the world is too much with us, we have to fall back on lighter topics. Today is such a day. After 10 days of a miserable flu, I just don't have the stomach for weighing in on the many layers of disgrace in Charlottesville. No "humorist" can take on such a depressing subject. And so I offer this.

On one of my last trips North on the 347 out of my DLV, I noticed that the hand-lettered Kettle Corn sign on the side of the road had added the cheery news: "Credit Cards OK." At last! Kettle Corn all around!

Now I am a big fan of entrepreneurship. And also a huge (and getting huger) Kettle Corn fan. But it will be a cold day in Hell (or even Arizona which has a similar climate) when I hand my card over to the smiley non-English speaking gentleman peddling stale snacks and "fresh" shrimp by the side of the road. What could possibly go wrong there?

Then I pondered further: who does not carry $3.00 in cash? Who needs to finance Kettle Corn? And, if you are in that dire of financial straits, would Kettle Corn not be a lower priority than, say, milk. Or tuna. Or even Top Ramen?

It sounds like a punchline to a Jeff Foxworthy "You might be a redneck, if…" joke. "You might be undercapitalized, if…you have to use a credit card for Kettle Corn." (My very favorite "Redneck" riff of Jeff's is "You might be a redneck if… you think a 401K is your mother-in-law's bra size…" Good one, Mr. Foxworthy.)

I believe that – IN GENERAL – men and women differ in their attitude toward carrying cash. Women, in my experience, prefer to use checks and credit cards. When I was a teenage clerk in my father's drugstore, it was not unusual to have a woman customer write a check for very small amounts, even under a dollar! Men never did this.

Women often seem to be a little scared of cash, either in the belief that they are more vulnerable to being mugged, or, more likely, that they don't trust THEMSELVES not to squander it faster than if they use credit cards or checks. Now, personally, I am much more cautious and reluctant to spend my cash than I am to whip out my plastic. Men, in general, will carry cash, sometimes in quite startling amounts. And I don't mean just criminals.

There are many people committing no crimes at all who are wary of the massive amount of government and corporate intrusion into our lives who prefer to leave as little a trail and live as far off the grid as is humanly possible. Everyone has Googled (spit, spit), say, patio furniture, and three minutes later got a pop-up ad for – what are the chances? – patio furniture! Which then appears every day for ten years. It is truly terrifying how many entities know every thing about us there is to know, including, but not limited to, our exact location.

The story may be apocryphal, but I once read that a major jewelry store in New York decided to send out thank-you holiday cards to men who had purchased expensive bracelets and necklaces on their credit cards. Which surprised the heck out of many wives who had not been the recipients of these gifts. Uh-oh. Whatever genius thought up that campaign must have been looking for work as a Salvation Army Santa by the time all the stuff hit the fan. Yet another argument for cash. And we haven't even yet mentioned strip clubs.

Once, in a particularly bleak period when Mr. AG and I were both between jobs, we had a credit card that was not maxed out, but no cash whatsoever. I don't know if we didn't realize you could get a cash advance on a credit card, but we didn't do that. Which meant that I could take all my laundry to an expensive dry cleaners and pay by credit card, but I didn't have a handful of coins with which to go to a laundromat.

The truth is that you have to have a certain level of wealth in order to practice thrift. When hamburger is on sale, my thrifty neighbor back in Minnesota will buy twenty pounds of it, make some into patties and fry up the rest for chili and spaghetti and bag it all for the freezer. But he needs the initial $95.00 or so in order to "save" money. Plus a big freezer. Lots of poor people don't have either one.

And I know that many struggling families budget very close to the bone. Once, when I performed at a Women's Wellness Night in rural Kentucky, the sponsors had advertised $3.00 in advance and $5.00 at the door for tickets. Several dozen ladies had misunderstood this and showed up at the door with exactly $3.00 and not a penny more. They were in danger of being turned away in tears when I insisted that they be let in and told the organizers to take the extra $2.00 apiece out of my pay. (I tell you this not to break my arm patting myself on the back for this very minor $50.00 contribution, but to avoid having to answer our favorite troll's daily inane "gotcha" question: "Why didn't YOU make up the difference, AG?" Answer: I did. And felt blessed to be able to do it.)

Which brings us back to that Kettle Corn. There is a very sentimental old union activist song called "Bread and Roses" with the lyric: "Hearts starve as well as bodies; give us bread, but give us roses." Maybe sometimes, a night out for comedy or a bag of Kettle Corn is worth your last $3.00. Go for it. But please. Not by giving your credit card to a guy by the side of the road. It may be embarrassing to explain to Visa that no, that full set of four radial tires in San Diego is not your purchase, nor the hefty liquor and entertainment charge at the strip club in Tijuana, but yes, that Kettle Corn is a legitimate charge. Three bags.

IT WAS THE STATUES!!!

August 25, 2017

Dateline…sometime in the not-so-distant future

Who knew? For many many decades the Educational Establishment had been absolutely consumed with the "gap" in educational achievement between students "of color" and students of extreme Nazi whiteness. And, of course, Asians, who are counted as "even worse than white" when it comes to curve-wrecking academics.

Some right-wing racists believed the gap had had something to do with studying more, fewer hours spent watching television, turning in homework, that sort of thing. But they were sent to reeducation camps and eventually were rehabilitated. The North Korean Get-Your-Mind-Right Diet Plan of 700 calories a day probably helped in focusing their attentions away from Wrong-Think.

Other outlawed Christian lunatics had noticed that there was a strong correlation between having a father in the home and the academic achievement and discipline of his children. The rations of such lunatics were reduced to 500 calories a day (2 yogurts, arugula, and a Fig Newton) until they came around.

So you can imagine their shock and dismay when these backward elements learned the truth: it was the presence of statues that had prevented black children from learning! The minute the offending statues came down, their SAT scores rocketed up, and the offending gap was erased. Or scores definitely WOULD have rocketed up if both letter grades and the racist, sexist, tests had still been allowed. Everyone who was not Irredeemable was certain that the gap was gone for good.

Nobody wondered aloud why The Lightbringer had had eight endless years to get rid of the statues and had not.

And nobody mentioned either that not one in ten students of any color knew who most of the offensive historical figures even were. At the time that the statues started coming down, 74% of all high school students identified "Andrew Jackson" as the 7th Jackson brother, the one that came between Jackie and Tito, and, sadly, the only one who couldn't sing.

"Thomas Jefferson" was described as "that President before Obama who slept with a slave or something" by 58% of students and "The guy who invented the telephone?" by another 25%. "Jefferson Davis" was believed by 48% of high school graduates to be "the real name of Snoop Dogg" and nobody even hazarded a guess about Nathan Bedford Forrest, except "a white guy who was bad?" (which turned out to be right, actually, proving once again that even a blind pig finds an acorn now and then).

When Mount Rushmore was dynamited and work begun on replacing the pale white dead men there with members of The View, albeit on a much larger mountain, little girls everywhere were so inspired by the sight that they flocked to science, math and engineering in record numbers. All the right people said so. (Fat Studies counted as a science major by then, even though "fat" itself had been entirely eradicated by changing the racist BMI charts.)

The sculpture of Crazy Horse, 17 miles from Mount Rushmore, a work in progress since 1948, was also dynamited. A few Native Americans complained, but they were overruled due to strong lobbies of crazy people who objected to being called crazy, and others objecting to the cultural appropriation of our equine companions.

The Museum of Science and Industry in Jackson Park in Chicago was offensive on so many levels that it was almost razed except for a last-minute reprieve by Mayor Lena Dunham, who had won re-election of the city of 2.7 million souls by over 5 million votes. She had lurked in airports reporting conversations she had heard and turning over her vast notes to the Perpetual Mueller Commission until she was elected to her first term just to get her out of airports.

Mayor Dunham – who often pranced about naked at her press conferences, reliving her Glory Days on *"Girls"*– convinced the public that Jackson Park was named for Jesse Jackson, Jr. who had set a national record for collecting disability. The Science Museum would be repurposed as a place to study Global Warming and other science-y things as soon as the Blizzards of '25, '26, and '27 could be cleared enough to get to it. Nobody liked "Industry" either on a personal or corporate level and so that stupid, racist word was dropped.

The oceans commenced to lowering and the unicorns scampered among the rainbows and all was right with the world after the great Statue Eradication Project of 2017.

YOU AREN'T IT!

September 1, 2017

I finally met a member of The Resistance in my Arizona! Well, I didn't meet her exactly. I saw her get into her car in the Walmart parking lot. Her Prius had two bumper stickers: the first announced: "Member Resistance: Resist Trump's Agenda."

Coincidentally enough, Mr. AG and I had just watched an amazing documentary called Above and Beyond, which I heartily recommend. It was about a Jewish-American World War II pilot downed behind enemy lines in Belgium. While trying to get back to his unit, the pilot traveled by means of 159 stolen bicycles. He was helped enormously by various local priests, and The Belgian Resistance whenever he could connect with it.

At no time did he locate The Resistance from one of them putting a bumper sticker on any bicycle or hay wagon bragging about membership in the group. The Nazi occupiers who served Actual Hitler would have appreciated such obvious clues. To be discovered was an immediate death sentence. Well, maybe not as immediate as one might wish. There would be torture to get other names first. Those Resisters were not virtue signaling; they were just virtuous. And courageous beyond my ability to comprehend.

Isn't it revealing how these present-day masked, marauding twits feel perfectly safe with Literally Hitler in the White House to publicly "out" themselves as Resisters? Does that not undercut somewhat both their status as courageous fighters battling Unspeakable Evil and their characterization of President Trump as Literally Hitler? This New Hitler guy must be a much more easygoing, relaxed sort of fella. In fact, these professional malcontents are merely poseurs pimping off the name and exploits of real Resisters who risked everything and often paid the full price.

The second bumper sticker was not just a childish and offensive posturing, but a large part of the reason President Trump was elected.

It said, "I have met 'the people' – and you aren't it." Cute. Talk about a desire (repressed, of course, I AM 70 years old, for God's sake) to key a car with: "You lost, loser. Get over it!"

Nope, we tens of millions of Trump voters are not "the people." This tolerant Resister has read us out of humanity. Oh, well, we're used to it by now.

First, we were characterized as The Bitter Clingers by Obama. Clinging to God – check; clinging to guns – check; "bitter" – no, every survey shows us happier than leftists; hating "the other" – no, that's you guys, but nice try. We don't even acknowledge that anybody IS an "other." It's YOU who invented all these categories of "otherness," we just see people. Maybe if you took off your idiotic masks, you could see people as people.

Then in the bizarre and hilariously mistaken belief that she could diss her way to the Presidency, we were attacked as The Deplorables, by Hillary. The Nazis preferred the term Vermin. We have had these kinds of names before in history. It did not go well for humanity.

So where to seek allies to defend our basic dignity? The media are a solid phalanx of hate for us and everything we stand for. Hollywood. Broadway. The Academy. Silicon

Valley.

Almost the ENTIRE GOP denied that first, Trump would win a single primary, then that he would get the nomination, then, of course, that he would win the general election. He was going to be "crushed by Hillary" said Jeb! with uncharacteristically high energy. Kasich sat out the whole convention in his home state of Ohio, refusing to be seen with the nominee. I would seriously vote for Mad Max Waters before I'd vote for Kasich. Better a babbling idiot who is an in-your-face open opponent of everything I stand for than a smarmy false friend with a perpetually snotty look on his face.

Perhaps our conservative friends who are regular invited guests and commentators on the political megaphone shows would defend us? No. On election night on ABC, there sat Bill Kristol, looking every bit as glum as his Democrat media friends as the electoral vote piled up for Trump. And some woman named Ana as the Designated Republican, cheering for "sweet justice" for Hispanics to get the credit for bringing down Trump.

I had so much respect for Bill Kristol, almost a crush on him because he looks a bit like Mr. AG. I subscribed to The Weekly Standard for years. I was filled with pride and gratitude, and called my mother to read her his kind words when he linked one of my columns. He even paid me once – actual cash money! – to review a book about the late, great author Donald Westlake, whom we both admired. I have no reason to believe he is anything but a nice man personally, although I do not expect to get any more assignments from him.

I believe the #NeverTrump campaign has done grave harm to the GOP brand and the flagrant obstruction of the Republican Establishment has so far stymied much – not all

– of the agenda we voted for. An agenda which the lemons we had elected previously pretended to support. Time and again, the Conservative wing has had to suck it up and rally round whatever centrist squish our betters put forward. And we did. There is no more reciprocity from that entrenched establishment than there is from the Democrats who believe that "bipartisanship" means that in every disputation, the Republicans just cave. Spellcheck should change the word to "buy-partisanship." P.J. O'Rourke long ago characterized that bunch as a Parliament of Whores, an insult to hard-working hookers the world over, who at least (I'm told) deliver the services they have agreed to provide.

DOG WHISTLES GALORE

September 8, 2017

Well, friends, I woke up this morning to a $1.00 bill on my nightstand. Now either that was a pathetic commentary on my contribution to the festivities the night before, or some kind of anti-Semitic "dog whistle" because, you know, money/Jooz, what else could that mean?

Then I remembered that I was cleaning out my wallet in my customary obsessive fashion, arranging the horrible dead white men's heads all going the same way, with the denominations in ascending order from front to back, and I decided to keep a single out to put in a birthday card for my friend, Barb, as a standing joke.

At least it wasn't a banana peel. Mr. AG, who is a runner, eats about three bananas a day for the potassium, and he isn't always meticulous about where he leaves the peels. He could single-handedly cause a campus riot. "Loose lips sank ships" in the War Years; now "Loose peels are Big Racist Deals" in the Snowflake Years.

Oh, Lord, have we FINALLY hit the bottom of the "triggering" barrel with a banana peel near a tree in Ole Miss? Because, really, I can't take much more.

Time and time and time again the terrifying little nooses and poop swastikas and KKK scrawls and "Faggot" cakes and hijab-pulling turn out either not to have at all or to have been done by an unbalanced attention-seeking member of the victim class at which it was allegedly directed. Both the great

Michelle Malkin and Ann Coulter have documented hundreds of such "incidents." Nothing EVER happens to the perpetrators. Down the Memory Hole it goes until the next psychotic meltdown.

The amazing thing about liberal guilt-wallowers is that it matters not a whit to them whether the "incident' happened or not. To their feeble little minds, it COULD have been real, and it almost-certainly happened once in history, so they are compelled to grovel and apologize and let morons scream spittle-flecked obscenities at them. Pledges are made to have MORE Diversity Drones and LESS scholastic accountability and MORE segregation and separatism and FEWER standards of decorum, even after the Great Banana Incident of 2017 turns out to be one lazy but semi-responsible person's attempt to make sure nobody slipped on his garbage.

Not one cowering, caving, college administrator or professor or – God, forbid! – aggrieved student ever says, "Hey, next time maybe we should wait until all the facts are in before we go bonkers." Heck no. Riot now. Repent in leisure, if at all.

Which brings us to the ever-present "dog whistle" theme.

It has to be THE most worn-out metaphor in 50 years (with the possible exception of attaching the word "Gate" to every new political scandal and crisis. Would that the Nixon-era DNC had headquartered in a Marriott instead of the Watergate. Then, the chyron for a new scandal in Boise could be tagged the "ID-iott" crisis.)

So a dog whistle is a high-pitched whistle that only dogs can hear. Usually it is applied to racist code words that few normal people have even heard of and that nobody can hear except the alleged racists – well, just them and every single Official Black Person appearing on CNN, MSNBC, NBC,

ABC, CBS and writing op-eds as the spokes-bigot of color who sees racism in every single human encounter. Now understand, their JOB is to detect racism on a molecular level; if they can find no racism, they have no job. They have great incentive to find racism everywhere. Most racism-detectors are woefully unqualified to do anything else, and certainly not at that kind of salary. I have no idea how former MSNBCer Melissa Harris-Perry's tampon jewelry business is coming, for example.

Van Jones is a particularly egregious example. He is a well-compensated avowed Maoist Communist, who evidently was discovered by Valerie "We've got our eyes on you, Van" Jarrett. His 2016 post-election analysis consisted of calling the Trump victory a "white-lash." Never mind that this made no actual sense for a number of reasons. First of all, the word he was riffing on is not "black-lash" but backlash, a word without color attached at all.

Second of all, when 97% of black voters voted for a black man for President, this monolithic voting bloc was called neither racist nor a "black-lash." But when some 60% of white voters voted for Trump, ONE OF the TWO white people running, we were racist bigots engaging in "white-lash." Hillary – who pandered to the mob in refusing to assert that ALL Lives Matter – was evidently given honorary non-white status. Which could not compensate for her unpleasant personality, grating voice, unpopular positions, Benghazi disaster, email destruction, influence peddling, fake charity, and failure to visit Wisconsin.

A significant percentage of those same dog whistle-hearin' racist white folks DID vote for Obama, twice, or he couldn't have won. Period. Naturally, white folks got no credit at all for that. There is no known way for a white person to prove he, she or xe is not a racist. Obama called his own grandmother who raised him in private school in Hawaii a "typical white person," by which he meant a racist. I wonder what it would take to make most normal people of any color diss their own Grandmas publicly.

Meanwhile, back to the scary, suspicious money on my dresser, I would hope to end with one of my all-time favorite jokes – undoubtedly sexist at a minimum for which I denounce myself in advance as I have learned from treasured Commenter Alasdair Burton. If I can somehow sneak this past my intrepid gentlemanly editor, Scott, it is pretty darn funny:

A man and his wife go to Vegas and lose a lot of money, including cashing in their airline tickets home. They discuss options and, given the dire emergency, the wife volunteers to work the corner outside the casino to get the $340 they need for the trip home. She comes back the next morning, exhausted, with $340.25. "Wow" says her husband, "You saved us! This is great! But, who gave you the quarter?"

"Everybody."

I'll be here all week…tip your waitresses…try the veal.

APOLOGIES: A HANDBOOK

September 15, 2017

Well, a talentless has-been who has recently inflicted herself on Australia and shall remain nameless, has retracted her weepy apology for being photographed with a grotesque bloody beheaded Trump mask. Color ME shocked! I totally believed she was sincere when she finally apologized after exhausting all other options and finding none worked.

Her best strategy would have been to issue a heartfelt, come-to-Jesus apology, especially to Barron Trump, live on the interest on her net worth of $20 million, then get out of the spotlight and keep her mouth shut for a couple of years and then gradually work her way back into the public eye, starting with charitable events for neutral causes. Americans are ridiculously-forgiving people. Marion Barry was reelected mayor after going to prison and being caught smoking crack with a lady not his wife, for Pete's sake.

But where's the fun in that for an aging, attention-driven brat? She tried a shotgun approach instead with multiple themes starting with the always-popular "I am a VICTIM – old white men have been trying to keep me down my whole life" to "The Trumps have broken me!" to "I'm sorta sorry" to the current "Trump has done way worse things and the reaction to what I did was BS and I'm BACK, baby. And P.S. I was never sorry. So there. Anyone who disagrees is a white supremacist." Very, very charming and mature for a woman in her late 50s. But nothing unexpected from a Mean Girl who made millions saying ugly things about the Palin kids.

Which got me thinking about apologies in general. As a Power Line public service, I will give you this little thumbnail sketch of apology etiquette to clip and save.

IN MARRIAGE

Your best option here is prevention. It's a terrible rookie mistake to allow yourself to be drawn into a discussion of 1) "Do you think this dress makes me look fat?" or, 2) Which of my girlfriends do you think is 'hot'?" Any missteps in either of these cases will result in an apology, extended time in the guest bedroom, and an extravagant gift. And there basically IS no answer to either question that would not be a misstep.

However, should a discussion be unavoidable – perhaps you've both had several Margaritas? — here are two answers. Memorize them. Then eat the paper.

Q: "Do you think this dress makes me look fat?" A: "There is no item of clothing that would make you look anything but beautiful, and you are even more beautiful without clothing at all." Do not be tempted to "gild the lily" by naming favorite parts and under no circumstances should you mention the word "thighs" and "the Donner Party" in the same sentence.

Q: "Which of my girlfriends do you think is 'hot'?" A: "Well, honey, I never see them when you're not around, and when you are around, there is only one hot woman in the room." (If you are lucky, it will be much later before she realizes this is a tad vague and possibly even ambiguous. Hopefully, you will be on a business trip to Cleveland or an over-the-road trucking trip to Bakersfield by the time she thinks it through.)

IN POLITICS

All sorts of unseemly things happen in politics, mostly because wretched, greedy, pathological liars with good hair are drawn to politics. Some of these things could require insincere apologies along the lines of "I'm sorry anyone was offended when I called half the American people racists. Even though they are."

But usually this unfortunate situation only arises if you are a Republican. If a Democrat's screw-up even gets reported at all (damn Fox News and those pajama-clad independent bloggers!), it will make no mention of party affiliation and be relegated to page 37 of the paper.

Let's say you get caught red-handed giving out the debate questions in advance to only one debater. You might think that you would be in some kind of trouble. Ask yourself: are you Black? AND a woman? No problem! Take a belligerent stance and face the camera proudly and say that you are a Black, Christian Woman and you won't stand for this kind of attack.

Let's say you are a white, male Democrat with no apparent victim category to shield you from a charge of fooling around. Uh-oh. But wait! With whom did you fool around? Woo-hoo! Have a press conference and announce to the world that you are "a Gay-American." End of story.

Perhaps you are a white male pedophile pervert who likes to use your small child as a prop when you text pictures of your bonerific Underoos to teenage girls. Because you are a Democrat – and, oh yeah, the husband of the First Female President's Best Friend Forever – you will be given a mulligan and you can even run for office again! New Yorkers are so sophisticated! It's not like you came from Oklahoma or Utah or something.

But here's the thing. And I cannot emphasize this part

enough, politicians. The behavior must STOP. If you do it
again, using the mortifying pseudonym of Carlos Danger,
and get caught again, possibly even impacting the election
of the First Female President, well, then you are toast. Now
you must attend costly sex addict therapy sessions, which,
for some reason, involve horses, and you must grovel, and
STILL your wife divorces you. You have no friends because
you are too stupid to live. If you are anyone other than
Anthony Wiener, you must now announce that you are
resigning to "spend more time with your family." Carlos may
even have to get a real job. The only Carlos I know shinnies
up palm trees with cleats on to trim the fronds. I could ask if
they're taking on any more help. It's dangerous work and
pays pretty well.

REGULAR PEOPLE

You have hurt someone's feelings, hopefully not on purpose.
Own it. Acknowledge it. Don't weasel around offering
excuses. Apologize for it for real. Ask for forgiveness. Don't
do it again. Accept forgiveness and continue on with your
life, humbled that you are forgiven and having learned to be
more sensitive in the future. Oh, and pay it forward – forgive
others when they hurt you. It is called, among other things,
"growing up."

EAT THE RICH!

September 22, 2017

Remember when Rachel Maddow had the big scoop of "somehow" getting hold of one of President Trump's tax returns? Never mind that every way of getting such a thing involved illegality. It was supposed to be another terrible strike against Trump that he, alone – unlike all other Americans – had used every legal loophole available to pay the smallest amount of tax possible into the giant, grotesquely-wasteful maw that is the United States government.

And then we learned that in that one year, "the smallest amount" turned out to be $38 MILLION dollars? Here's what I – and probably at least a few other ungreedy people thought: that should be IT. He's one and done. Here's your receipt, sir, and thanks for your massive contribution. Thirty-eight MILLION, are you kidding?

Leftists, Sandernistas, Millenials who've never paid in anything in their lives but think everything should be free, are howling: "Are you serious, AG? But, but, but… he's RICH. Think of how much he's MADE in America? He should pay more! Lots more! MILLIONS more!" Why? They can never articulate that. Just that it isn't "fair." Obviously, someone that rich "deserves" to be perpetually hosed by the tax system in order to support "The Poor."

But, see, he HAS supported hundreds, probably thousands of people, actually PREVENTING them from being poor. Think of how many people he has hired in his long business life. Think of how much he has paid in to Social Security for all those employees. It would be a staggering figure. And then, of course, there's the "trickle down" amounts – just to take one example, all the lunch counters and hard hat and work clothes emporia around his construction projects.

Of the 47 percent who pay nothing, zero, bupkiss, nada in federal income taxes, for millions of them they not only do not contribute; they are simultaneously a terrible COST to society. If you are a never-married woman with two boys and a girl from two or three different deadbeat "fathers" (sperm donors, for all practical purposes), not only do you get food stamps, cash welfare, Section 8 housing and Medicaid, but without a father on-site, there is a very good chance that one or both of those boys will end up incarcerated at a nominal cost of $50,000 a year per. And the girl could beat the odds and become a successful "Website designer" like the famous "Julia," or she could start cranking out fatherless babies of her own at age 14.

I remember an episode of Phil Donahue years ago that featured ONE Puerto Rican woman from New York whose giant extended family of welfare recipients was costing the taxpayers a cool million dollars a year. Yes, you read that right. This episode could surely not even be aired today. It would be "blaming the victim," "punching down," "raaacist," "sexist" and "slut shaming," just for starters. I'm sure I'm leaving something out.

Veering off temporarily in an entirely different direction before coming round again, it was my privilege to get to know a family of legal Jewish immigrants from The Ukraine. The young man and wife were each about as big around as my thumb due to actual starvation in the Workers' Paradise from whence they had fled.

The mother of the woman was a vegetarian, as she had given any small scraps of meat they were able to procure to her daughter and her husband for the protein. When the young woman, let's call her Nadia, shopped an American supermarket for the first time, she got dizzy and nauseated at the ludicrous profusion of food. She had to use her hands for blinders around her eyes and run to the produce section where she found a cabbage and three potatoes, familiar food, and proceeded to the three-minute checkout line.

They were all very intelligent ("cognitively privileged"), trained in I.T., including the mother. They all got jobs and eventually, after a baby arrived, they bought a small house. They told us that they pretended still to be renting, because they could not tell even their closest Ukrainian friends they owned the house. The Soviet system was built not just on terror, torture, and routine Lena Dunham-style spies, eavesdroppers, and informants, but on massive envy.

Nadia said that in America, people do not hate the rich because — until recently — everyone thought he had a shot to one day be, if not rich, at least comfortable middle class. But in the FSU, they were taught to hate anyone doing even a little better. She told us a Russian joke she said was representative of the Soviet thinking: a man was told by a genie that he could have anything he wanted, but whatever he got, his neighbor would get double. After thinking for a minute, the man said, "Just blind me in one eye."

When we see virulent, hateful campaigns and riots against the One Percenters – financed, with no apparent irony, by Soros, a .0000001%er – it is a harbinger of great trouble ahead. The pro-socialism Bernie campaign, indeed the fact that he may well have prevailed without the Hildebeasters gaming the system, speaks volumes about the human propensity for greed and envy. You add in the "white privilege" drivel, and you've really got trouble.

Why in God's name, is it considered noble to want to

confiscate a big chunk of what your neighbor earned, but the height of greed to want to keep most of what you earned for yourself?

You watch, my friends. In the unlikely event that President Trump is not hamstrung by the RINO Witch Trio plus John "The Maverick" McCain*, you are going to hear more screaming than a spoiled toddler at Toys R Us. "Waaah…Trump's tax reform is just for The Rich!"

The economy is doing better than it has in 8 years. The President has just hit the "unattainable" 3 percent growth in GDP, hoping to exceed that, and the lockstep Democrats and their Republican collaborators simply cannot allow that to happen. Why, what would the voters think? They might never vote for either party of thieves, liars, lawless open borders fanatics, gun-grabbers and grandstanders again.

*Media Stylebook: Note well, John McCain is a "maverick" when sabotaging his own Party. When he tries to run for President, especially against The Light Bringer and Lowerer of Oceans, then he is just another run-of-the-mill racist, sexist, homophobic hate speaker whose very presence caused Whoopee to leave the set of The View lest he sell her into slavery.

NANCY PELOSI: HOMESPUN

PHILOSOPHER

September 29, 2017

I suppose it is a matter of opinion whether or not it is constitutionally permitted to engage in Nancy Pelosi's infamous shouting of "Wolf!" in a crowded theatre. Personally, I believe it is, although it may hinge on how the Wolf chooses to be addressed.

But I can promise you shouting "Wolf" or "Javelina" or "Gnu" is unappreciated once the feature film begins. Cellphone users and shouters of random animal names in a Minnesota theater – crowded or otherwise – are liable to meet with the Minnesota-approved severe "half-turn with pursed lips," precursor to the dreaded "full-turn with shaking head, more in sorrow than disapproval." Because the only sin in liberalism is being "judgmental."

Mr. AG believes that I could match Mrs. Pelosi aphorism for aphorism as one of my lifelong favorites has always been "I'll burn that bridge when I come to it," a reference to my habit of stomping off several jobs without having other employment lined up. It's probably hard for my loyal readers to imagine, but your Ammo Grrrll used to be something of a hothead.

Thank goodness I spent the last 30 years of my working life SELF-employed as an entertainer. I was born to be self-employed. And asked to become so on numerous occasions. And even then I failed to ever win "Employee of the Month" even once. I'm so congenitally anti-authoritarian that I couldn't even take orders from myself. If I was supposed to write a new routine for a corporate banquet show by Saturday, and it was now late Thursday night, I would feel an urgency to alphabetize my spices instead.

But I digress from the topic at hand, which is the incomparable wit and wisdom of Nancy Pelosi. Fresh from her triumph as champion of illegal immigration until the Dreamers ran her off the stage, she opined that illegal immigration was an act of love if small children were involved. And how about armed robbery if you promise, swearsies, to buy toys for your kids with some of the loot? Let's take a stroll down Memory Lane of Nancy's Greatest Hits.

In one famous YouTube presser two weeks into President Bush's second term, some Democrats were gathered in a diverse little clump, as is the custom. And Speaker Pelosi – front and center – said there was "nothing, nothing" which she could work on with the President because his promises were "a hoax. A hoax." Even Mad Maxine Waters turned around to look at the colleague behind her with a "WTF?" look on her face.

Nancy has also gone charging to the other side of the famous "aisle" in order verbally to attack Congressman Tom Marino (R) Pennsylvania. She must have nearly capsized Sen. McCain (D-Arizona) whose chair is IN the aisle, the better to stroke Schumer's, uh, hand. Nancy was shrieking repeatedly that Marino was "insignificant." At which point she was restrained and removed by the Sergeant at Arms, who must get as much work as the much-ballyhooed Maytag repairman of yore.

These displays and many unhinged orations have raised serious questions about her mental or physical health. We may be looking at an entirely new definition of "Nanny State," i.e., a Syndrome in honor of Nanny Pelosi, characterized by freezing up and repeating some mindless phrase like a broken Chatty Cathy doll whose string has been pulled too many times.

And so we look at some of Rich Nancy's words of wisdom, fit for a Poor Richard's Almanac. I stipulate in advance that some of the "quotes" may not be 100% accurate, a technique I learned is perfectly kosher from every single dealing I've ever had with "journalists." Some are direct quotes and some are what I'm pretty sure she really meant. I also include a feature that Poor Richard missed, which is my own response to some of her real statements. So off we go, and enjoy!

"The Boy Who Cried Wolf in a crowded theatre was eventually burned to a crisp when the firefighters never came because he had yelled Wolf instead of Fire too many times."

Building on her infamous "We have to pass the Affordable Care Act to see what's in it," she later is reputed to have said, "Let's buy that gazillion-dollar dress before we try it on."

"If everybody had free health care, nobody would need to work and we could all become poets. Like that Emily Lazenfuss who built the Statue of Liberty and wrote that beautiful poem for it. 'Give me your poor, your tired, your tubercular masses and let them huddle in somebody else's neighborhood.'"

"It's not the size of the Speaker of the House, it's the size of the great big stupid gavel she is shlepping."

"Remember, a frown would just be a smile upside down if it weren't for Botox."

"And by the way, THAT was an applause line." (Oh, honey, I learned the hard way that if you have to TELL your audience to laugh or applaud, you have already failed...AG.)

"The poorest people in America are infants and children! Infants and children!" (Yes, Nancy, their net worth is appalling, and job discrimination against them is rampant, the infants in particular. AG.)

"What a terrible thing it is to lose one's mind."

"Oh wait...that was poor Dan Quayle having one of those brain-freeze moments we have ALL had, trying to remember the motto for the United Negro College Fund. Sorry, Nancy, you can't get credit for every great turn of phrase, though this one is a singularly appropriate classic.   It now pretty much describes the entire Democratic Party.

OCTOBER, NOVEMBER, DECEMBER

Fall in the desert is particularly beautiful. There might still be some days in the 100s in October, but the nights will be comfortable enough to open the doors and let the evening breezes come in through the screens. The snowbirds wend their way back from their summer homes in Canada and the Northern States and welcome-back parties are held on patios.

Sadly, the very first column of the 3rd Quarter of Ammo Grrrll Year coincided with the bizarre and still unsolved Las Vegas terrorist attack. There was nothing funny or even enlightening to discuss, but I did cull out four "Girls Gone Stupid" statements during that week, one of which got a woman fired from her law firm. She suggested that the horrific murderous attack was okay because, in any event, most country western fans were Republicans who owned guns. Nice. The Democrats always keep it classy.

The next week we learned from multiple sources that Harvey Weinstein liked having lovely young women watch him shower. Whatever. While disgusting, it really couldn't compare with a Democrat woman articulating that killing country western fans on the off-chance that they were Republican was fine with her. In fact, most of the columns from the Fall Quarter revolve around mounting examples of a psychotic breakdown among Democrats. I tried to find humor in some of it, but I confess to a good bit of anger and near-disbelief. And they were just getting started. Maybe get yourself a good stiff drink or a whole chocolate cake before reading most of the columns in this section. Maybe both.

The quarter does end on a reasonably-humorous and upbeat note with 12 New Year's Resolutions. And as our yearly odometer turns over to "2018" we say goodbye to the first crazy, bitter year of the reign of "Literally Hitler" and the unhinged response to losing an election by millions of people who should know better.

GIRLS GONE STUPID

October 6, 2017

I will not be commenting – except indirectly further on – on the monstrous evil in Las Vegas until more facts are known. I am writing this on Tuesday, must submit it for editing on Wednesday, so by the time you are reading this, anything I have to say about Vegas will either be too late and discussed ad infinitum, or too early and since disproven.

I'm sorry; there will be nothing funny today. The horror is too recent. Maybe next week. And so, in somber reflection, I will discuss instead some of the cultural landmines that are detonating around us to contribute mightily to such a catastrophe.

I will cite the recent comments of four women. They are acutely embarrassing to my gender, which is probably how righteous men feel when they see cringe-worthy video of a 250-lb man in an elevator slugging his girlfriend with a closed fist.

The first comes from former First Lady Michelle Obama. Weighing in on Hillary's pity party book signing, she opined that women did not listen to our "inner voice" telling us to vote for the candidate with the uterus. Most paranoid schizophrenics set great store by voices. But I guess my inner voice was too busy telling me to vote for the candidate who MIGHT secure the border, protect Israel and preserve both the First and Second Amendments. Hillary was 0-4 on all my issues. Michelle also said that those of us ladies who favored President Trump did so solely because our menfolk told us to. Yup, nailed it! I have no opinions until Mr. AG tells me what they are. Ask anyone who knows me.

Young Conservative commentator Katie Pavlich dispatched the retired Lunch Lady Scold deftly with one Tweet: "Does this mean that all women should have voted for Hillary against Obama in the 2008 primaries?" #GameOver.

The second woman who disgraced herself in the last week or so was that moronic librarian who rejected Melania Trump's gracious gift of many books, including several by Dr. Seuss. She wrote a snotty and condescending – not to mention totally ludicrous – letter to the First Lady rejecting the books because they were – what the hell ELSE in 2017? – RAAACIST.

Of course, since "the Internet is forever" (a great new song by Brad Paisley), we quickly saw not only Mrs. Obama reading Racist Dr. Seuss books to children, but the racist librarian herself dressed up as none other than The Racist Cat in the Racist Hat.

We have sailed into this "intersectional" gibberish territory of tribal loyalties and an ever-evolving pecking order of "Professional Victimhood." We have left entirely the traditional safe harbor of "E Pluribus Unum," of love of America, and even of basic MANNERS. In terms of manner, I am old enough to remember a time when a snarky public repudiation of a nice gift would have been considered as bad as telling the President that you would have to "think it over" before accepting an invitation to the White House to be congratulated on your sports championship. Mr. Curry, Mr. Kerr, I am so sorry I rooted for you. It won't happen again.

Of course, no natural or man-made disaster can occur, no victims be yet cold, without the pudgy potato-shaped little pedophile, Lena Dunham, weighing in. Here is her brilliant analysis of the Las Vegas mass murder: "No way not to politicize this tragedy. It's about gender & race as well as access to guns." What – no "homophobia"?

Well, yes, there WAS a gender component to the event in Las Vegas. Several self-sacrificing MEN deliberately took bullets for their beloved – and even random – women. Oh, it was a white guy who did it this time, and that makes it about race? How come you disgusting hypocrites NEVER say it's about race when it's a Somali Muslim or a black convert to Islam beheading a white co-worker, or a psychiatrist of color at Ft. Hood or a wretched Muslim mother who just slaughtered the people who threw her a baby shower? Weird how this guy who did, in fact, kill black people and Hispanic people who were also country music fans, killed mostly other white people. How does that work if you're a white racist?

Which brings us to our final Un-American Woman of the Year, the CBS lawyer, now looking for work. Ms. Hayley Geftman-Gold, of Columbia Law School, Tweeted that she was "not even sympathetic to victims of the Las Vegas shooting because "country music fans often are Republican." I particularly love that "often." Paul Mirengoff has written beautifully about this disgrace and its aftermath and several hundred commenters have added much to the discussion. To VERBALIZE that sentiment was beyond stupid, but what in God's name would even make her THINK it?

A dear friend of mine had a severely disturbed teen. Once when I was over at their home, she deigned to arise at the crack of noon and went foraging for food. Finding some chips but no dip, she let loose with a blistering volley of profanity directed at her father. Embarrassed to death, he asked me quietly later what would have happened to me had I said that to my Dad as a teen. I said, "You mean when I got out of the hospital?"

But that was a joke. Daddy only smacked me once in my whole life, which I richly deserved at the time. I explained that it was neither fear of him, nor even respect for him, that would have prevented such a verbal assault on a parent. IT

SIMPLY WOULD NEVER HAVE ENTERED MY HEAD!
Sorry about the ALL CAPS, but I think it's that important!

When a gaggle of prominent Minnesota Democrat women told me after 9/11 that "America had it coming," it began my transition from left to right. When famous people Tweeted that they wished Steve Scalise had died and taken many other Republicans with him, when Ms. Geftman-Gold can say "go ahead and fire into a crowd of country music fans because most of them are Republican gun-toters," then America is truly lost. Those sentiments are the direct result of Alinsky calumny, fifty years of anti-American education, and repulsive identity politics. The refusal of Hillary, Bernie and other politicians to say "All Lives Matter" is not just craven kow-towing to the thugs in BLM. They actually do not believe that they do.

SEX STUFF: MEN AND WOMEN MAY BE DIFFERENT!

October 15, 2017

As even casual readers of this column know, Mr. AG and I have been married for a very, very, extremely very long time. Because Mr. AG knows me so well, he does feel that he can correct me if I have something terribly wrong. You know, for my own good. So I don't make a fool of myself. Especially in print.

But sometimes I am right. Like in this conversation over breakfast a few days ago:

Me: Did you see the most recent revelations about Harvey Weinstein?
Mr. AG: You mean beyond the many women he mauled, harassed and, possibly, raped?
Me: Yeah, that, but, I'm talking about the allegation that he wanted them to watch him shower.
Mr. AG: Hahaha. You must have that wrong, honey. You mean he asked to watch THEM shower!
Me: No. What I said.
Mr. AG: (Uncharacteristic long silence and frowny face.) That can't be right.
Me: That's what several of the women say.
Mr. AG: Where's the fun in that? Is that a thing?
Me: Apparently just another thrill we never heard of. Who knew just watching a big, fat, wet, hairy guy wash could make him so happy?
Mr. AG: Yuck. I'm eatin' here…

Oddly enough, I feel kind of sorry for Harvey, who, on top of everything bears the name of a very large, nasty recent natural disaster. Maybe that's how they picked the name. Oh sure, he sounds like a disgusting, bullying,evil, sick Democrat puppy who took "casting couch" to a new dimension, or at least to a new room in the house. But two things leap out at me and make me suspicious.

First, the many many actresses and assistants now coming forward, apparently did not feel it was important enough to mention to the authorities at the time if it might damage their careers. Like the 40 or 50 drugged Cosby victims, they made a choice. Among other things, of course, this allowed other women to be abused, too. According to some reports, there WERE women who tried to approach the law and were shut down. Exactly how far does this rot go?

But, I also do "get" the idea that if someone has the wherewithal to land you a role that will get you millions of dollars, or PREVENT you from ever working in Tinseltown again, even as a barista at Starbucks, you might be willing to play Shower Cam or drink that Rum Roofie. And that is one of the rare occasions when the word "privilege" might be apt – "white" in Harvey's case, "black" in Cosby's. But mostly just "rich, powerful and connected" privilege. Plus, the icky guy probably weighs over 300 pounds, three times the size of the average anorexic actress. A lot of MEN would have trouble fighting off someone that large and mean.

But, second, why now? Cosby had made a target of himself speaking out against pathologies in the black community. But how did Harvey find himself suddenly in the crosshairs? He was a money spigot for every pet Hollywood cause — friend and pal to both the Clintons and the Obamas. Surely he embraced and funded every cause the New York Times held dear. What, besides the Times' reflexive anti-Semitism, would make them decide to go after one of their own in such an embarrassing fashion? I think more will emerge in the lawsuits and counter-lawsuits. He must have groped the wrong woman somewhere. Why him, why now, especially since his piggy behavior was an open secret in Hollywood for decades? Stay tuned.

I know men like sex. Cool. Who doesn't? But, seriously, guys, what's up with all the pervy stuff? Beloved male commenters: Help me out here. Are there a lot of you who think, "Boy, if I ever get rich and powerful, I'm going to ask a woman to pretend to be a young pet owner while I dress up like a hamster. I'm building my own man-sized cage right now with shredded newspaper on the floor"? (OK, bad example, cuz, who hasn't done THAT?) But a lot of these creeps sure do have some weird fetishes. Personally, I think once you separate sex from love, and commitment, you need ever kinkier stuff to get a kick. Like needing higher doses of drugs. But that's just me and I'm admittedly a Grrrll.

Rich, powerful, but unattractive, men must be in Literal Hog Heaven when they find they now have access to gorgeous women who wouldn't have given them the time of day in high school and now can be made to do literally anything for money, ambition, or fame.

But how men decide that the high they get from their particular proclivities are worth risking everything for, that is a phenomenon most women do not understand. I mean Anthony Weiner was even given a mulligan and he went right back to the behavior, albeit with the clever disguise moniker of Carlos Danger.

From that married politician repeatedly texting pictures of his swollen undies to teenagers; to a famous married spokesman for a sandwich company looking to have sex with young boys; to a married President of the United States playing with cigars and an intern in the Oval Office – these men and countless others have wreaked havoc in their lives for extremely fleeting pleasure. Mystifying! Women do terribly self-defeating and destructive things for what they imagine to be "love." But just for sex? Meh. Maybe throw in Chicken Fried Steak, Biscuits and Cream Gravy and a piece of warm Rhubarb Pie with Praline Ice Cream, now we're talkin'.

And now Harvey is in Full Damage Control Mode, gathering prominent feminist attorneys and Maoist PR flaks around his bulky (but evidently, very clean) body. He's being schooled on spouting the correct gibberish by the best feminist scolds. But best of all, he is going to channel all that former sexual energy into – wait for it! – GUN CONTROL! Yes, he can't control his gonads, so he's taking his raging, aging hormones and his liberal libido to the perpetually-slandered NRA. And just in time too. I wonder what Paul Sorvino thinks about Harvey going after his daughter or Brad Pitt thinks about this sleaze puttin' the moves on his wife. Maybe it IS time to "talk about Fight Club."

A word of advice, Harvey, on your new cause . If you ask one of those righteous NRA ladies to watch you shower, you could have considerably fewer parts to clean in the future.

THE OLD BOOKS

October 20, 2017

As I have mentioned several times before, long ago in a galaxy far far away, I — like many a foolish youth before me — was a card-carrying left-winger. That was one of the MANY reasons why I was so unimpressed with candidate Obama. I had seen his "community organizer" type a hundred times before. Lazy, glib, shallow, narcissistic, and not nearly as smart as he thought he was. I was, however, almost alone in thinking he wasn't even a very good speaker. I still don't. (I once mentioned to my dear, late Mama that I couldn't stand Obama's fake Southern preacher voice and cadence and she said, "I wouldn't know. I just hit MUTE the minute he comes on." Ah, she was a pip. Wish you all had known her.)

Anyway, in the early '70s, I traveled with some of my cohorts to a convention of radicals in Milwaukee for some kind of Peace and Freedom conference. At one point, a group of us looked in on a room with a literature table for the National Welfare Rights Organization.

Now I will happily stipulate that I was a naive, political IDIOT at that time, but to my limited credit, even I thought that was a terrible name for an organization. I was enough of a conservative at heart even then that I did not believe that anyone had any kind of "right" to welfare. Maybe a need for it for a short period of time, but as an act of mercy, for which the recipient should be profoundly grateful, not as a permanent lifestyle or entitlement.

A bunch of us were standing around a table staffed by some

younger activists and a couple of older ladies. It soon became obvious from their rhetoric that they were either members of or influenced by the Communist Party. (It's a bit "inside baseball," but, trust me, the rhetoric of all the political sects at the time had various verbal tics and "tells.")

One of the older ladies started talking about Papa Joe Stalin – I do not make this up – and what a wonderful, kind leader he was and how much his people loved him. One of the younger activists looked embarrassed and said, "No, Ethel, that's not right. Where did you get that?" and she said, "It's in all the books."

And then came the money shot and the theme of this column: "NO, HONEY, THOSE ARE THE OLD BOOKS." Oh, how quickly those "books" are updated, expunged, airbrushed and condensed. Or just plain burned, if necessary. Along with their authors.

You would think it had been decades ago that candidate Mitt Romney was mocked and fact-checked for saying in a debate with President Obama that Russia was a concern. Ha ha ha, what a crazy old anti-commie lunatic! "The 80's called, Mitt, they want their foreign policy back," quipped the spontaneous Obama speech-writer into his ear wig. And the media lapdogs just licked Obama's face or wherever in happy agreement that that was THE most clever comeback anyone had ever heard.

How could it be a short four years later that the Ruthless Russkies were guilty of everything from kidnapping the Lindbergh baby to preventing Hillary "Uranium Saleswoman of the Month" Clinton from being crowned? Bwaa-ha-ha! All that influence-peddling, and no influence!

But Putin did not act alone in ruining everything. No, the evil, terrible, no good, very bad James Comey also colluded and connived and was a key player in keeping Hillary from punching through that glass ceiling and therefore, Comey is Satan (since Hitler is already taken) and he should be drawn and quartered and the parts arrested and…WAIT! WHAT? Comey is FIRED??? Hitler can't fire Satan, can he? Our Comey? The gentle giant of the FBI? Those were the Old Books from last month!

Various feminist "comedy" shows (def: bitter, angry screeds that take great care to include nothing humorous) and other cultural offerings were strictly For Women Only. Now feminists aren't even allowed to use the title "Vagina Monologues". Not because the concept is old and kind of repulsive (like many of the audience members), but because it is hurtful to "women" who do not have a vagina. Not only are those early feminist ideas from the old books, but the women who wrote them, once heroes and pioneers, are rapidly being read out of the movement. Evidently they aren't "woke" enough. Maybe too much decaf; who can say?

When pre-Candidate Trump yukked it up privately (ha! As if anything were private nowadays…) 11 years ago with Billy Bush, telling the gospel truth that rich men attract gold-digging women who will put up with anything, including being grabbed, the Outrage Machine got cranked up to "eleven." Out of the woodwork magically appeared several women, many of whose stories did not ring true to me. (And I must say I am not overly-impressed with SOME of the current crop of actresses who suddenly remember an actor committing one random boob-grab two decades ago.)

But the Left knitted their Pussy Hats and asserted that all women must be believed again, which was a stunning departure from the Clinton Years when it was open season on Trailer Trash women who came forward. Led by The Wronged Wife, soon to be a carpetbagger Senator from New York, a campaign was waged to vilify, slander and mock these women. Who did they think they were, anyway? Hint: Not our kind, dear.

Old books; new books; it is dizzying trying to keep up with when and which women MUST be believed and which are to be dismissed out-of-hand and made into late-night punchlines. Why, some feminist bigshot whose name escapes me – I could look it up, but really, who cares? – even claimed all women should be honored to put on their Presidential kneepads in gratitude for Horny Willie protecting the liberal sacrament of abortion.

It's all #WarOnWomen every election unless outing a Democrat serial predator might interfere with #TheWarOnBabies. Then it's Kneepads all 'round.

THE AMERICAN MUSLIM RESPONSE TO TERRORISM

November 3, 2017

It has happened again, of course, and will again. A lunatic Muslim Uzbek, here on a "Diversity Visa" – which, I thought had to be a made up thing, but no, it's real – has killed many people, wounded more. At least the name Sayfullo Habibullaevic Saipov is probably not going to ring through the ages. Let's just call him So Full O' Sh*t for short. I'm sorry he wasn't shot dead or run over like his fellow-terrorist "Speedbump" Tsarnaev of Boston Marathon fame. Sadly, U.S. taxpayers had to foot the bill to operate on So Fullo's gutshot stomach, and will have to house him forever if the feds don't succeed in cutting it short with capital punishment. He's only 29. That's a lot of coin.

What do American Muslims think? The silence is deafening except for the tedious routine of handwringing about Islamophobic reprisals. Yeah, yeah, I know we don't exact group punishment in America or demand group disavowal. Except for white people and gun owners, we don't attribute to all members of a class or race the actions of the worst of them. ALL white people are racist in their DNA according to a certain half-white President whose white half was the one that raised him in privilege in Hawaii when he was abandoned by the black Muslim half. Oh, well. Hillary was more measured in asserting that only HALF of us Trump supporters were Deplorable. How gracious. No wonder she won.

A Republican candidate for dogcatcher makes some asinine

statement about women or gays or whatever the Protected Category du Jour is, and the Democrat press has to wear Depends to keep from wetting themselves as they shove microphones into the faces of every Republican they can round up to force them to "disavow" the miscreant.

To my certain knowledge, not a single Democrat was asked if he agreed with texting pictures of one's distinguished member to teenage girls, but then sexual disgraces are resume enhancers, not embarrassments to Democrats. When Slick Willie's dalliance with Ms. Lewinsky was revealed, Bill Maher opined that he felt sorry for poor Clinton because his playmate wasn't as hot as JFK's Marilyn Monroe.

But where, oh where, are the daily microphone forests surrounding Keith Ellison to ask his opinion of Manchester, Paris, Barcelona, the London Tube attacks or the NYC truck attack? Why has he – or that Somali Muslim woman in the Twin Cities who unseated Phyllis Kahn, DFL State Representative for Life – never been asked to speak on the record about female genital mutilation?

But even more mystifying, why have the several million adherents of The Religion of Peace in America never, not even once, had a big public demonstration against terrorism? Could it be that they don't actually disagree with it? Or that they are genuinely "phobic" about their maniacal Islamic co-religionists, living in fear of being beheaded, burned alive, crucified, drowned, thrown off rooftops for being gay, and such?

I remember at the height of the Iraq war, with American soldiers fighting to liberate Iraq from Saddam, I saw on TV a table with several cute little Muslim high school girls in their modest dress circulating a petition. I think it was in Michigan, but I wouldn't swear to it. And I remember thinking, "Oh, isn't that great? They are supporting the war effort."

But, no. They were petitioning to "protect" the mosques in Iraq, asking their fellow Americans — soldiers only a few years older than they were — to be especially careful not to harm the damn mosques. To hell with the soldiers who had to fear enemy fire coming from within the precious mosques. And schools. And "baby milk plants." They had no concern whatsoever for the soldiers, only for buildings. And I thought, "In what sense are they Americans?" It is one thing to oppose the war for real, if misguided, differences of opinion. Americans can and did disagree. But it is quite another to worry only about places of worship – all rebuildable – rather than the safety of American troops. Can you imagine Christian teenage girls in World War II petitioning to ask their brothers and fathers and uncles and classmates to take extra risk to their lives and limbs in order not to harm churches?

Did the Somali community of "Minnesota Men" mobilize to isolate its jihadi wannabes, to say loudly and publicly to the authorities, "Thanks for weeding out these troublemakers who give the rest of us such a bad name"?

Absolutely not. All demonstrations were raucous displays of tribal loyalty for the "rights" of the guilty-as-hell young men. Community leaders made additional demands which can be subsumed under the general heading of "Gimme." Gimme more welfare; gimme more midnight basketball, gimme more poverty pimp money; gimme expensive and useless programs to bribe our brain-dead young losers not to become terrorists.

Hey, remember when your ancestors reached these blessed shores from Norway, from Poland, from Russia, from Ireland, how the first thing they did after signing up for Section 8 Housing, Food Stamps and Medicaid was to demand wheelbarrows full of money in order to bribe their sons not to blow their hosts to Kingdom Come? No? Me neither.

I want to see a giant demonstration of Muslims in Washington demanding an end to international terrorism. I want there to be contingents from Muslim Army veterans, contingents made up of allies from the synagogues and Christian churches just like that bumper sticker that says "Co-Existence." I want to hear every speaker at the rally saying, "Terrorism is WRONG! Stop murdering in our name." Period! No mealymouthed "justifications" (thank you, Kerry and Barry) like cartoons or grudges against Crusaders, the last batch pushing up daisies since 1291, give or take.

And I also want a cure for cancer and a once-a-day pill to take that will allow me to eat anything I want in vast quantities and not gain weight. Care to place odds on which of these things will happen first?

DON"T CARE WHO "LOOKS LIKE ME"!

November 10, 2017

When I was a kid, back in the era of the single black rotary wall phone and the kerosene guitar, we could watch sporting or cultural events and appreciate the performance rather than obsess over bean-counting the race, gender or sexual orientation of the performer. What wonderful innocent days! How much we all have lost with wretched identity politics.

When I was in junior high, my beloved grandfather, a World War I vet and hardcore South Dakota Republican, once showed me his John Madden-type Dream Team of all-black baseball players. He probably called them "colored" then. He loved baseball and he admired talent. Although he was born in 1891, and undoubtedly believed several backward things — such as that a man found lurking in the ladies' room in a dress and lipstick is a man who will soon be punched in the lipstick -- he was as fair-minded as the day is long. For him, talent trumped skin color.

The other night, Mr. AG and I watched an interesting history of the comedy clubs in New York and Los Angeles. It was fun to see George Carlin with neat hair and a suit and tie and Jerry Seinfeld as a scrawny young kid in long hair. One of the last people featured was a lovely young black woman, a comic just starting out, who said she loved doing standup. As a 30-year veteran retiree I thought, "I would love to mentor her." And then she said, "I wish there were more people who look like me." I have heard this phrase repeatedly in recent decades and wondered how it ever got such a strong toehold. It never resonated with me or even made much sense. How would that behoove you in any way, young lady?

I can look in the mirror any old day if I want to see "someone who looks like me." In fact, exactly like me. Why would I ever have limited my role models to short, pale, tomboyish girls?

In truth, darn few people I watched or admired "looked like me." John Wayne and Gary Cooper had the right to trial by jury in common with me, but not a whole lot else, and I loved them both. They – and pretty much ALL the cowboys we 50s kids were raised with –- taught me courage, independence and fighting back against bullies. If "High Noon" does not teach us what one righteous person can accomplish by standing firm, then nothing does. It never occurred to me that that lesson did not apply to me because Mr. Cooper was more than a foot taller than me, male, and rather better-looking!

I delighted in welcoming the Twins franchise to Minnesota in 1961. My three favorite players were Harmon Killebrew, Earl Battey, and Zoilo Versalles. I failed to notice at the time that I admired a white slugger whose grandfather was the strongest man in Idaho, a black catcher and a Cuban shortstop. None of whom looked like me except in an x-ray.

As you can guess, I loved comedy from an early age and would memorize routines to do for my friends, whether requested or not. But the routines I loved the best involved exquisite timing: Jack Benny. Bob Newhart. Early Woody Allen.

I loved Minnie Pearl and Phyllis Diller and later admired Joan Rivers, but I never felt they were any more "role models" than the male comics just because they had lady bits like mine. I learned Bill Cosby's "Noah" routine word for word, with its catchphrase delivered by a resonant God, "Noah, how long can you tread water?" Clearly, I had little in common with Mr. Cosby then, and even less now, as I have only rarely been forced to drug a sexual partner unconscious, which can only end in severe disappointment for the woman.

My little ol' country Mama's (b.1921) favorite song when I was very young was Nat King Cole's "Mona Lisa." One of my earliest childhood memories is of her switching radio stations repeatedly, hoping to find it. She had not a racist bone in her body and loved people whether they looked like her or not.

My own musical taste runs from Brahms and Mozart to Gladys Knight, Sam Cook, and The Temptations; to Kiri TeKanawa, the Maori opera singer; to Ella Fitzgerald; to The Eagles, Toby Keith, Don Williams, and Brooks and Dunn. And, of course, the Beatles. Who looks like me in any of those groups? If I don't stop overeating, I may soon look more like Pavarotti or Meat Loaf than Stevie Nicks. But why in the name of all that's Holy would I limit the lifelong daily pleasure I have received from music to only small Jewish women artists? You can only listen to Janice Ian's "At Seventeen" so long before sticking a fork in your eye.

Identity politics pretends to be about "diversity" but it is about power. In a textbook case of "irony," what identity politics really does, quite simply, is shrink one's world down to a bland, cultural desert consisting of only people who can check all the same boxes as we do – black, gay, urban woman, for example. Exploring any other culture, befriending any other humans, eating unfamiliar food, all those things that actually EXPAND our worlds are verboten. Either it's cultural appropriation – another of the most vile, stupid concepts around – or "Uncle Tomism" if a black guy likes Brad Paisley instead of rap, or even along with rap.

And, of course, the list of boxes representing trivial things that divide us grows ever larger, as the circle of tolerance for differences gets ever smaller, until that circle looks like one of my quarter-sized groupings from plinking. Haha. Little boastful gun joke there.

Jewish women are unwelcome in leftwing anti-Semitic feminist circles; long-time feminist warriors find themselves read out of the movement unless they accept and embrace "women" without vaginas. And on it goes. Some moron asserted that heterosexual black men are the "white men" of the Diversity World. Good grief! "No man is an island," wrote poet John Donne, but the leftist loons are working hard to make every American isolated, envious and enraged.

Meanwhile, I intend to be joyful and content. And to continue eating tacos, Massaman Curry, Thai Potstickers, and brisket, wearing hoop earrings, listening to reggae and the wonderful Mexican music my housekeeper's young son listens to with guitars and a tuba. (Example: Ulices Chaidez, Te Regalo, YouTube it! Especially if it might annoy the "cultural appropriation" crowd.) I plan to associate with whomever I please whether or not they look like me. The Talmud asks, "Who is wise?" and answers, "Who learns from everyone."

I refuse to be put in a box. Because history has shown us that the next thing that happens when you allow yourself to be put in a box is that some tyrant nails down the lid.

DYING IN THE STREETS FROM HITTING THE GLASS CEILING ON THE PLANTATION

November 17, 2017

When I was young, Art Linkletter had a book and a show called *"Kids Say the Darnedest Things"*. Leftists say the darnedest things too, apparently in the belief that if you just say them often enough and loudly enough and with enough spittle flying from your mouth, that they will become true. For today's Friday Fun, let's examine just three of these moronic phrases.

THE GLASS CEILING

Oh, gosh. Ladies could be anything except for that darn glass ceiling. We try and we try and we are allowed to get so high and then, WHAM! We bang our heads on that pesky glass ceiling. Let's leave aside the fact that I can walk without stooping on a very small plane and have never hit my head on any ceiling. Since childhood, I have accomplished every goal I ever set, despite being a grrrll. Are these women up on 12-foot ladders wearing stilettos when they hit that glass, or what? Men, on average, are taller than women. Wouldn't THEY also bump their heads on that ceiling or does it somehow only cover women?

And, then, if you are lucky, you break through that ceiling! Which sounds downright dangerous. If you DO break through it, won't it shatter and spray you and the people below it with shards of glass? That seems like a pretty good description of what has happened when loony women like Maxine Waters, Frederica von Eavesdropper, Sheila Jackson Lee, Patty Murray, Nancy Pelosi, and, Miss Uranium herself, Hillary Clinton, have broken enough of the glass ceiling to inflict great harm on the hapless people below.

Besides, it's a crock. Women are astronauts, construction workers, pilots, surgeons, lawyers, senators, engineers. And have been some of these things for a lot longer than Affirmative Action has been around. I once entertained a small trade group of Women Electricians. It broke down pretty neatly into two types of members: the first, a group of tough, righteous "old broads" (a term I use with the highest respect), who had gotten into the trade through a family business; and the second, a few young women who had won places at the table through Affirmative Action. Would it surprise you to learn that the women who had done it on their own were not overly impressed with the new forced-hires?

We have had plenty of dreadful to mediocre male Presidents to be sure. But there are really only two women I have ever seen on the national stage whom I would have voted for to lead the country – Condi Rice and Jeane Kirkpatrick. And neither one because she was a woman.

DYING IN THE STREETS

The wretched actor, faux comic, and political "activist" Russell Brand, to take but one example, has shrieked at some length about the terrible medical care in the U.S which leaves "the poor" to "die in the streets." Well, no. Most of "the poor" who have the brains to sign up are covered by Medicaid. The rest go to the ER with a cold because they can't be turned away. Name one person scooped up from dying in the street, unless it was a victim of a gang drive-by in gun-controlled Chicago.

On the other hand, in Mr. Brand's native Great Britain, people die in the halls of filthy, neglected hospitals or are given "palliative" medicine if they are too old and sick to merit any further care. The difference in breast cancer survival rates in both countries is appalling.

A friend of mine in the Canadian NHS waited two years for a hip replacement, hobbling around in great agony while he waited. He was wintering in Palm Springs when his name finally reached the head of the queue. He had one week to get back to Canada to claim his place. If he demurred, he did not go to the next available spot. Oh, no. He would be put at the bottom of the queue again. An American friend wintering in Phoenix decided she had had enough of her hip pain. One week later, she was in Rehab recovering from the surgery.

I remember reading during the Obamacare debate that at one hospital in Colorado, two mentally-disturbed homeless men had cost the ER department over two million dollars because they rushed to the ER with "heart attacks" night after night, and the staff had no choice but to take their "symptoms" seriously. Should one of the men actually have a heart attack on the 27th trip, after being sent away, distant relatives who hadn't seen Uncle Henry – or was it Horatio? Whatever – in a decade, would descend on the hospital with the Colorado version of Gloria Allred seeking "justice" in the form of a boatload of money. For them.

In America, nobody "dies in the street," but you hear it all the time as a talking point.

THE PLANTATION

Oh, how I would LOVE to bring back Frederick Douglass or Sojourner Truth to hear Jesse Jackson claim with a straight face that "picking cotton" as a lifelong chattel slave and "picking footballs" for millions are exactly the same thing. (Picking footballs? Do you mean interceptions? So only cornerbacks and safeties are slaves? What the hell are you babbling about? Talk about a tortured analogy.)

Grow up, Jesse. What a pity you couldn't have found one of your catchy rhymes for "football" – "loot Mall"? no, best not go THERE – but even you know better than that. Slavery was one of the most cruel and wretched institutions in the history of the world. That it still goes on in the Middle East and Africa is rarely, if ever, noted. Perpetrators are the wrong colors and wrong religion. Not to mention that I consider drug dealers of any color to be the modern version of slavemasters. Their slaves OD in junkie dens or cars with babies screaming in their car-seats, and the dealers get new slaves whose every hour is devoted to one thing: get more drugs!

Yup, the NFL is just one big plantation. Show up for 16 Sundays, maybe a Thursday or Monday, get $12 million a year (minimum of half a million), get more for endorsements, live like a king, go clubbing with $8,000 bottles of champagne, drive drunk, beat the heck out of the child of one of your six baby Mamas, knock your girlfriend silly in an elevator. Sounds exactly like Uncle Tom's Cabin to me.

When you hear any of these inane phrases, call bullcrap. Enough, already.

NOW IS THE TIME FOR ALL GOOD MEN...

November 23, 2017

On an hourly basis, we learn of another woman making accusations of sexual harassment, assault, even outright rape. Other women claim to be "uncomfortable" or offended by a hand on a shoulder, a pat on the back, any human touch. I come from a warm "touchy" family, so I have tended to believe that a lot of those complaints are overwrought. But then I sat down and thought about my own experiences and got depressed. I wondered if ANY female person escapes unscathed? I am pretty tough, worldly, and unusually impervious to locker room talk, and still it's not a pretty picture. I warn dear readers that what follows is a downer and I'm sorry. I will be funny again next week. And yet I feel lucky. I have seen only my husband in the shower and we own no indoor potted plants.

When I was nine years old (1955), I spent a Sunday afternoon at a friend's farm near a lake. We played outside all day and in the late afternoon went down to the lake. A man who was well known to us was there in his fancy speedboat. He asked us if we would like a ride. Woohoo! Sure! Then he said that the very large boat was "too small" for all of us and he could only take us one at a time.

I was a logical little girl even then and it was obvious to me that the boat would hold at least six. Alarm bells went off, but I was so innocent I didn't even know what to fear. I had been warned of Stranger Danger, but the man was not a stranger. He took me first. Somewhere in the middle of the lake, out of sight of the shore, he turned off the motor and my little heart sank. I thank the dear Lord that what he did, though disgusting and terrifying, was not as bad as it could have been. He made me promise not to tell, under threat of being thrown overboard. I could not swim. It took me 20 years to lose my fear of deep water.

We came back to shore and I tried to warn my friend without alerting the monster. Shaking my head "No" and trying to use my eyes, I said softly, "Let's just go play." But, naturally, she wanted a turn too. For decades I harbored guilt that I had failed to prevent her abuse. He did exactly the same thing to her. Afterwards, we ran to the farmhouse, crying. Her mother realized something was terribly wrong and asked us what had happened. We told and a virtual bomb went off. She ran into the field where her husband was on the tractor. He ran back to the house and called my father. Though the farm was about 8 miles from my house in town, Daddy showed up in less than 10 minutes. With a loaded shotgun, God Bless him.

They separated us and questioned us intensely, lest we were just two imaginative little girls making stuff up. Our stories were identical and unshakeable. They got in the car with two shotguns and went to the man's house. He denied it, but our Daddies said if they ever saw or heard of him coming within a mile of their daughters again, that they would kill him. I told; I was believed. Daddy took care of it. I learned that there were bad men and good men who would protect you. I also learned always to trust my instincts, my gut. A forever lesson.

I have been treated to two flashers who would have been well advised to stay covered. One while jogging and one while waiting for my then-boyfriend in the living room of his college dorm. I called the police on the one outdoors, because when a man outdoors is naked from the waist down, one can never be sure his intent is not more serious than exposure.

A very boring, repetitive obscene phone caller bothered me a couple of times a week for a year until we figured out who it was. This was long before Caller ID. The worst part was that the idiot always called right after I had finally drifted off to sleep from my night job. I dared not take the phone off the hook, lest I miss an emergency with my son or parents.

I called the cops and a nice officer came right out and took me very seriously. He assured me that the vast majority of these pathetic losers are not dangerous. When we finally figured out who it was, I had my good friend Randy, a Vietnam vet, call him. He told the guy that he had been a Green Beret and if he ever called again, Randy would see to it that he would never walk right again or be able to dial a phone. The calls stopped.

Those are the actual crimes. The rest falls under "hostile work environment" which I consider way, way, way less serious. Feminist friends sported "I believe Anita" buttons. My problem with Anita Hill was not that I thought that she was lying; I thought that if every single thing she said was true, it was still a giant nothing-burger. Some stupid jokes about Long Dong Silver? That's all you got? She was never touched and followed Justice Thomas to every job.

When I worked night-shift with the 80 guys, I could not possibly log the nightly suggestive comments and kind offers they felt I couldn't pass up. Truly, most fell into the category of harmless banter, and some were even funny. I either gave it right back to them or ignored them. Though never groped, I was often slapped on the behind. Could I have whined to the bosses? Of course. In my family, tattling was never rewarded. And, secondly, I was the only woman in this shop, a pioneer. I wanted to prove women were tough enough to handle it.

Only one thing upset me in three years. On an older

co-worker's birthday, he asked me to kiss him on the cheek; I attempted a chaste little peck at which point he turned his head, grabbed me and stuck his tongue in my mouth, Franken style. I screamed, "HOWARD!!," and pushed him as hard as I could. He fell over a chair. The other guys cheered. He went home early.

In my 30-year comedy career, no club manager, corporate client or fellow comedian ever got out of line, except for one subsequently-famous comic, usually high on cocaine, who used to beg me routinely: "Susan, please, just show me one [slang word for breast]." There will be no weepy news conference in which I out this sophomoric chucklehead with Gloria Allred by my side. If it had upset me unduly, I would have kicked his sorry butt myself. On the other hand, he IS very rich now... No. There are some contexts in which if you can't take the heat, you should get out of the kitchen, and a comedy Green Room is definitely one of them.

But what about that little nine-year-old girl? After moving to another state to drive a school bus, the pedophile was eventually arrested for molesting his own grandchildren. He is long dead now, looking forward to brunch this Sunday with Charles Manson. I wish Daddy had shot him in 1955. I wish I could bring him back from the dead to shoot him now.

Can you good and decent men – *whom I count in the vast majority* – not somehow police the monsters? Every last lefty Hollywood "man" knew about Harvey. Every. Last. One. The moral cowards, busy Tweeting about the Republican "War on Women" stood by and were complicit for decades. Give me my "redneck" father and his shotgun any day. As Richard Pryor intoned, decrying racism by parodying a Psalm: "How long, O Lord, must this bullshit go on?"

LOOPNER NATION

December 1, 2018

Last week I talked about some very serious, very real sexual crimes. Today I want to look at the potential for disaster in believing every ancient accusation out of hand, without proof.

Back in the Bronze Age when Saturday Night Live was funny and the fabulous Gilda Radner, of blessed memory, was still alive, a recurring skit concerned the "Nerds" of the Loopner Family. Sadly, Mr. Loopner, who, for obvious reasons we never see, was "born without a spine." Who knew he had sired millions and millions of children despite his serious disability? I am astonished and embarrassed by the utter lack of "spine," "grit", or real COURAGE of so many of our fellow citizens and nearly all politicians.

The masked fascism fighters who mock the courage of soldiers, firefighters, and police officers risking their lives every day are knocked aside like a twig swatted by Godzilla by a Twitter swarm. What's with the masks, anyway? What cowardly, pretentious twits! I attended several large Tea Party rallies with nary a mask in sight. Sure, a few Colonial Army tri-corner hats, the occasional fife and drum, but no masks. No need to hide our identities. We planned to commit no crimes. No bicycle locks with which to whack people who were lined up to hear a speaker we hate, no arson, just leaving the area cleaner than when we arrived. For which we were dubbed the derogatory name of a sex act by Anderson Cooper. What a card, that guy!

Thank God the Brits didn't have Twitter as a weapon when General Washington was crossing the Delaware. We might be speaking English now, calling trucks "lorries" and elevators "lifts" and eating vegetables that have been cooked for a minimum of 5 hours.

I had thought for just one horrible moment that I would have to say something positive about Lena Dunham who, for a nanosecond, defended a friend accused of a rape that allegedly occurred years earlier. But, before I even got my computer booted up, she folded like a cheap cardtable and recanted. Not that there was the slightest danger, but I'm glad I don't have to count on her as a friend.

How do we learn courage? Where do we learn to stand up to the mob? Not just the violent mobs that the Reverend Dr. Martin Luther King and thousands of brave black people and white supporters faced. But the one formed by the cool kids in high school who will say nasty things about you that go viral and later not invite you to their Georgetown parties.

I learned a lot about courage from my Mama. Small lessons that left impressions. She stood an inch above five feet, weighed about 98 lbs. soaking wet. She was a little toughie, a dead-eye shot hunting, a South Dakota farm girl who could break an apple in half with her bare hands. She was always picked first when we chose sides for a sandlot softball game: "WE get Mrs. B. You guys have to take Susan. Put her in right field. Way out there. Further."

Standing up to the crowd was child's play to Mama. She was the only lady in the neighborhood who reached out to and befriended the new woman who moved in across the street. Gerri had a slight drinking problem and – are you sitting down? – was DIVORCED. Yes! Hard to believe now, but that was a big deal in 1958 small-town America. I think the poor woman may even have had her ears pierced. The Slut Trifecta!

In Memphis during Wartime, when Daddy was stationed there, Mama took a part-time job at a department store. At lunchtime, the clerks and secretaries would eat bag lunches in the company cafeteria. She noticed a black janitor always eating alone, and joined him for several days in a row, until another employee warned her that, not only would people call her hateful names, but that she could put HIS very life in jeopardy if she didn't cease and desist.

But back to the loopy Loopner-esque Ms. Dunham. Her dreadful thoughtcrime was to doubt an accuser until further evidence. That is not allowed in Leftist World. Women NEVER lie about rape, asserted this clueless Tweet Queen. They lie about what they had for lunch, she joked, but not rape. Well, then, we've already established that they do lie, haven't we? Have you weighed them and checked their Driver's Licenses? How short is our collective national memory? She herself had a specious claim of rape in college and yet dares to opine!

We have the Duke Lacrosse Team disaster in 2006, complete with the 88 disgraceful faculty lemmings who acted as judge, jury and executioner in condemning the innocent young men whose lives and reputations were ruined. Before that, of course, we have the Tawana Brawley case in which a young black woman, encouraged or enlisted by Al Sharpton, charged 6 white police officers with smearing her with feces, and tossing her in a trash bin after raping her. None of which happened. So not only is a woman capable of lying about rape, but she is willing to smear herself with dog crap to make it credible.

We have the UVA fraternity hoax with a psycho ninny making up a lover out of whole cloth and then claiming he organized her gang rape. At least she cost the despicable Rolling Stone magazine when they wrote about her laughably-improbable tale. There were eight other college fake rape stories about the same time. Eight!

These are the famous incidents of fake rape accusations. In just my own life, I knew a then-young woman with a strict father. One night in the small town I grew up in she was coming home past her curfew and knew she was in trouble. She got out of her car, rolled in the dirt, tore her clothing, and told her father – and later the doctor and police – that she had been raped by 3 black men, who had been passing through town. It was all a pathetic tissue of lies which fell apart almost instantly under investigation. (Later, she was fired from her job in a nursing home for stealing money and jewelry from the aged residents. Nice gal!)

I know at least two women who falsely accused exes of molesting their own children in bitter divorces. Really, does it get any worse than that? Not for nothing does bearing false witness rate a particular mention early on in the 10 Commandments.

Men lie. Women lie. Children lie like rugs. Rose McGowan I believe. Ms. Tweeden I believe, even without the grotesque photographic evidence. But I have grave doubts about some of the #MeTooers. Mark my words: Turning America into a perpetual Salem Witch Hunt where any man can be destroyed just by accusations of incidents that allegedly happened 40 years earlier and can never be disproved will not end well. Ask not for whom the 10, 20, 30-year-old sexual assault accusation tolls, my brothers; it tolls for thee.

CHIMING IN

"The horrible thing about the Two Minutes Hate was not that one was obliged to act a part, but, on the contrary, that it was impossible to avoid joining in." — George Orwell in the novel, 1984.

Georgie said a mouthful there! We see it with the attack on Taylor Swift now for failing to chime in on hate for Trump. I will return to this in a bit.

When I left my little left-wing sect in 1979, I lost most of one set of friends. In fact, unbeknownst to me, the group voted specifically to disinvite me to their convention held every other summer at Oberlin. I had had no intention whatsoever of going, but they felt it was necessary to make sure their members got the message that any deviation on their parts would result in similar shunning. A powerful social control tool, that. Used by all cults, political or religious.

I remained a left-of-center Democrat for over 20 more years, basically until 9/11. When Senator Paul Wellstone – who had made a MAJOR pledge to serve only two terms – announced his intention to run for a third term and turned out to be exactly like any run-of-the-mill lying, promise-breaking politician, I bolted to the Republican Party. Naturally, he had to break the promise because he was such a "fighter" for us that he felt we needed him.

I don't know about you, but I really don't want any politician to fight for me; I just want him to get out of my way and leave me the hell alone.

When I not only supported Norm Coleman against Wellstone, but became his speechwriter, you can imagine the hue and cry in my group of die-hard leftie Jewish friends, almost every last one of them a very nice person. They believed that we had simply lost our minds.

Now in case there's any reader who does not know that Minnesota is as Blue as an Antifa delayed-adolescent holding his breath because Trump is #NotHisPresident, let me remind you that Minnesota is the only state (out of the Obama 57) that didn't go for Reagan either time. I made my living entertaining corporate, women's, and trade groups all over this great land, but probably at least 30 percent of my business was still in my home state of Minnesota. Which was an easier commute in any event.

One morning, I fielded a phone call from the male president of a professional psychology group looking for entertainment for an upcoming national meeting to be held in Minneapolis. This would have been in 2002 or 2003, during W's first term. In our conversation, certain cues made me picture a balding, grey-ponytailed guy. We had a pleasant chat, and he even became kind of flirty, despite my mentioning my husband several times. Things were going swimmingly as we were about to close the deal. We discussed the venue, my fees, how much time he wanted me to fill, where to send the contract and the like. Then from nowhere he said, "If you could work in some material about this effing war criminal Bush, it would be great."

Uh-oh.

I said, "Oh, I don't really do politics in my act. It usually alienates one half or the other of my audience. It's just pretty generic humor that can unite us all and get us laughing."

Long pause. Then, noticeably more frostily: "Well, in THIS

organization, that won't alienate anyone."

"Ah, I see." I can feel my chickens evaporating before they're hatched.

And then, "You DO agree, don't you, that that effing idiot is an effing war criminal?"

Sigh. "Sir, I really hate talking politics with potential clients, but, no, I think it is slightly more complicated than that."

Click. It was the first job I lost from failing to chime in, but far from the last.

Whenever I hear lefties whine about McCarthyism and the so-called "black list" (which I'm pretty sure is now a racist term...), it makes me laugh. Yeah, yeah, like every single pendulum swing in human history, some people who were not "commies" but only sympathizers, got swept up in the desire to clean out the government and unions of real card-carrying Communists whose stated goal was to overthrow the government of the United States. But thousands of them were actually guilty as hell. My sympathy is limited.

Ask James Woods or the tiny handful of other conservatives in Hollywood how many jobs they have lost. And now, as we said at the beginning, Taylor Swift is being virally hounded, not about supporting Trump, Land O' Goshen! (as my grandma used to say), but about failing to chime in on hatin' on him.

Ms. Swift's net worth is reportedly somewhere between $280 and $380 MILLION dollars. If she never worked another day or sang another note, she couldn't spend the interest on that, whichever one it is. (I love the discrepancy in Website estimates of more than $100 million dollars, a small rounding error, I guess, in that financial ozone layer.)

I hope she holds firm and resists the bullying. Talented, smart, gracious, pretty, AND an inch below six feet tall, I am in awe. And green with envy on the height thing. If only we could do a kind of socialist "redistribution" of height, split the difference, and we could both be 5'6". I would be so much thinner!

BUY THIS! BUY MORE!

December 15, 2017

Well, it's just days until Christmas and the shopping frenzy is in full swing. I have often thought that – were we a proselytizing religion, which we are not – we Jews could set up booths and recruit at Malls during the stressful Christmas season. We would just have to keep it on the down low, until we sign them up, what an observant Jewish housewife is obliged to do during the eight days of Passover. (Hint: just one small part is going through every book you own looking for "chametz" or prohibited leavened crumbs you might have dropped, eating a granola bar while reading. We own thousands of books.)

Those kinds of rules and the pork prohibition seem to be quite the deal breakers for many people. Personally, I like Turkey Bacon just fine, but I have heard it compared to "eating a Band-Aid." With a preference for the Band-Aid.

I have read that fully 75 percent of all toys sold in this great and good land are sold at Christmas. That's an astonishing statistic and makes me wonder why the big box stores even bother to keep toys on the shelves for the rest of the year.

Every year there seems to be an effort to proclaim such and such a toy is the one children cannot live without, causing scarcity, and such festive Christmas traditions as stabbing other patrons in line in order to get the last Tickle Me Elmo. I have, of course, seen the bumper stickers and wristbands asking "What Would Jesus Do?" and I'm pretty sure that "When celebrating the day of my birth, slay thee another parent who seeketh to grab the last Cabbage Patch Doll" was not part of The Sermon on the Mount. I could be wrong. I'm no expert on the New Testament…

This manufactured scarcity was the occasion of my one and only shining moment as a Super Hero several pre-Amazon decades ago. My former karate teacher in San Francisco, then living in Victorville, had a little 5 year old boy whose very life depended on acquiring at least one of the Power Rangers. He had searched all of California and even Arizona and Nevada. He thought maybe Minnesota kids weren't as hip as California kids and the craze had not yet hit there and called me in desperation. He was mistaken.

I spent several days on the phone calling Targets and K-Marts in towns small and large throughout Minnesota. I called clients in Georgia and Alabama who had girl children (sexist!) and was told by one that if I found a female Power Ranger, she would pay me $100 for it.

Finally, a K-Mart clerk in Duluth found not one, but FOUR different Power Rangers. It was like she had found The Ark of the Covenant! I gave her my credit card number and told her to throw in a $25 tip for herself, which she said she could not do. The package arrived. I examined the toys from every angle, trying to see what all the fuss was about and, failing that, wrapped them in Christmas paper and Fed Exed them on to my friend and sensei. He told me later that his son was the Big Dawg in the neighborhood for months to come and that he would never forget me. So I got a 10th Degree Black Belt and former Army Ranger guy on my team should the need ever arise. Word.

I love how many industries have creatively ginned up a way to use vast amounts of their products. Try reading the recipes on cereal boxes: "Take eight cups of Rice Krispies…"

A comic I worked with 35 years ago – Sid Youngers – used to have a very funny bit (I'm going to guess he isn't using it any more…) about how baking soda convinced us to put an open box in our refrigerators and, having wild success at that, to pour a box down the drain! Talk about using up product – just buy it and throw it out!

Big Pharma simply gives trips and perks (and probably crack and hookers!) to doctors to convince us to take more and more drugs for maladies they invent like Restless Leg Syndrome and Social Anxiety. Plus they keep moving the goalposts, defining as problematic the very numbers that were considered ideal just yesterday. Like "High" blood pressure is now 120/80. Did you know that? I looked back at old annual checkup sheets and saw I had a Happy Face sticker on a Fasting Blood Sugar number that has now been reconfigured as "pre-diabetic." (Really, isn't EVERY number below THE "diabetic" number "pre-diabetic"?)

Just the other day I was reading about how one should throw out one's kitchen sponge EVERY WEEK to avoid contamination with harmful and icky germs. That came as a surprise to me. I generally threw them out when the "scrape-y" side became too useless to do a good job on pots and pans. Leave it to Big Sponge to try to force people to buy 52 sponges a year! Likewise with Big Makeup. I have also read articles in ladies' magazines that advise us to throw out all our makeup and especially mascara and other eye makeup every 3 months.

Is there anyone out there who actually does that? Deb? Tracy? Dorothy? Colleen? Anybody?

Here is my idea for saving even more money on makeup: don't use it. Same with hairspray, nail polish and almost all face creams and potions. Nail polish is absolutely destroyed when shooting or cleaning guns. I have seen women with hairspray that could, conceivably, deflect bullets, but I've never worn a hairstyle that required the helmet look. If you are married to a man who thinks you look better with pale green eyelids, well, that's your call.

Happy shopping and a Joyous and Blessed Christmas, Hanukkah, or Winter Solstice. Stay out of Malls and Walmarts on the day AFTER Christmas when half the stuff you just indebted yourself to purchase gets unceremoniously returned.

HYSTERICAL LOSERS

December 22, 2017

Recently, my friend and colleague Mr. Hinderaker and many others have addressed the relentless and bewildering hysteria of the opponents of every single thing President Trump is doing. It gives every impression of a mass psychotic breakdown.

Why should this surprise anyone who has been paying attention for the last five years? When "rape" is defined as "having totally consensual, if drunken, sex, and deciding afterwards that it was assault because he didn't return your 37 texts the next day"; when "harassment" is one pat on the behind you remember from 30 years ago; when "racism" is a banana peel in a tree or wearing hoop earrings, then how could hysteria not be involved?

In November, as is the tradition, an election was held. A man won; the other candidate lost. And a highly-paid, major newscaster who a few hours earlier had predicted a landslide for Hillary, assured her viewership, "You haven't died and gone to Hell. This is your life now." Shockingly, one candidate has lost in every single election since Washington. Why the over-the-top freakout? I have some ideas.

Most of the people losing their minds are not nearly as bright as they think themselves. However, they are the rich, the spoiled, Life's perpetual "winners" who are unaccustomed to losing and loath to get used to it. Especially to a bunch of nobodies who have never even once been in People Magazine. Ah, but you say, Trump is hardly a nobody. True. But, no matter how much they insist otherwise, it isn't really

Trump they hate. It's those of us Bitter Clingers who voted for him.

"How could I not be 50 points ahead of this guy?" asked Hillary. And her media and Hollywood admirers seemed to say, "But, but, but, I have been told my whole life how special I am, how on earth did my heroine lose to voters from icky Kansas and Mississippi?"

"Waah, waah, waah," cried the losing losers. "President Obama, of the creased pants and ocean-lowering abilities assured me that I was on the right side of History." History disagreed. That History can be a real bitch on wheels, eh? And not for the first time.

Nobody – probably not even Mitt Romney — was more sorry than I was when Obama was reelected in 2012. And rather handily at that. Here's how prescient I was, how plugged-in, how "finger on the pulse" accurate I was – I truly believed that Romney had it in the bag. Oopsie. Call me Karla Rove. (And pay me what Karl gets to opine.)

So my candidate lost in 2008 and again in 2012. Did I lose my mind? Did I scream piteously in front of a cellphone camera that "I need an ambulance RIGHT NOW! I'M NOT KIDDING!" as one unhinged college girl was captured shrieking last November? Did I shed a single tear? No, I did not. The sane among us just bought more ammo and tried to be happy as revenge.

In 2007, in San Diego, in one of my last gigs before retirement, I entertained a group of public employees. My presentation followed a Global Warming Hysteric from the IPCC, being paid God-knows-what. I was pacing around in the back of the room, listening to his droning drivel. In the Q & A, one effete young man asked with tears in his eyes and a quavery voice, "How much time do you think we have left?"

and I had all I could do not to scream out, "Oh, for God's sake, kid, get a grip!" But it's really bad form for the next speaker to attack the presenter on stage or mock a member of the hiring group, no matter how close to retirement one is. Manners and all that.

We are now over 10 years on. Virtually all of the overblown predictions have melted much faster than the polar ice cap and I'm guessing that the terrified little fellow has found another cause to be hysterical about. No doubt involving #NotMyPresident, Literally Hitler, DJT.

Okay, we get it, people. You do not like Donald J. Trump. But when you say LITERALLY Hitler you display your willful ignorance about the meaning of "literally" and you trivialize the real record of the Third Reich. To someone whose husband's extended family had eleven people murdered in the Holocaust, comparing a tax reform plan you don't care for to systematic mass murder is offensive to the point that I would like very much to punch you in the face.

A year into the Trump presidency, it goes without saying that there are no death camps. There are no mobs of White Supremacists rampaging through black neighborhoods. I can show you mobs of Black "youths" swarming Walmarts and beating random white passersby thought to be Trump voters. I can show you masked Antifa fighters of various colors whacking the elderly, torching cars, blocking freeways, preventing invited speakers from getting to their venues on college campuses. I can show you meltdowns of serious, "unbiased" newsreaders and celebrities du jour calling for the impeachment, beheading or death of a democratically elected President.

Our millionaire Democrat news-heads reported breathlessly when President and Mrs. Obama had a date night and when the family went out for ice cream. Both were major news items. No such luck for President and Mrs. Trump to get a nice little human interest story. The media have publicly and collectively vowed not to "normalize" him or his family. Stop the presses! Trump gets two scoops of ice cream when everybody else gets just one! And we hate the White House Christmas decorations even more than we hate Christmas! And Melania wears beautiful high heels to a hurricane! As the saying goes: you couldn't even make up crap this trivial and mean-spirited.

Though I am writing this on the 8th night of Chanukah after a Festival of Light and Latkes Party, it will be read just a couple of days before Christmas. It goes without saying that most of the left-wing lunatics are not interested in a Holy Night, but perhaps, mercifully, there might just once, be a Silent one. Merry Christmas to all my Christian commenters and friends.

RESOLUTE OR DISSOLUTE?

December 29, 2017

In just three days the year will roll over to 2018. This is kind of a disconcerting number for me because for 38 years, that was my house number in my St. Paul suburb. Feels weird for it now to be a date. My hand will automatically add "Kenwood Drive" after 2018.

I am determined this year to make a series of Important Resolutions and keep them. I will share the Top Twelve with you because Top Ten is such a cliche. And invite you to share some of yours.

One. I resolve to offer a couple of politicians — Jeff Flake and Susan Collins are already taken — $2.00 apiece to get them to vote against something I haven't read but have been told I must hate. I don't know what the dollar threshold is when an offer officially become a bribe. Needless to say, I cannot match Rosie's $2,000,000 apiece offer and I wonder how awful someone's life could possibly be who has $4,000,000 to fritter away? Poor Rosie O'Donnell seemed like a nice person until she turned out to be batshit crazy. I met her when I was on her VH-1 Standup Spotlight Show in 1991. She was kind to me and seemed like a sweet kid. Oh, well. It took ten more years for her to go off the rails and become a 9/11 "Truther." Then Trump's election put the final nail in the coffin of her mental health, as it has with so many others. Sad.

Two. I resolve to sit less. We keep being told that prolonged sitting is just as unhealthy for us as smoking. So, since there is no difference, I have decided to smoke instead of sitting. I will pace vigorously around outside office buildings with the other pariahs and we will have the last laugh over the non-smokers sitting for hours at their terminals, as their muscles and organs turn into a gelatinous, but self-righteous, blob.

Three. I resolve to clean all my guns. Since my rotator cuff injury, I have been shooting less than I used to. A lot less. Feeling that I'm not putting that many rounds through the weapons, I have not been as conscientious about cleaning my guns. It's embarrassing. I will clean them just as soon as I locate the instruction manuals for each one, as I have also forgotten how to field strip all but two of them. Sigh. Is there anyone in the Phoenix area who would clean guns for really great Brisket? (Just asking for a friend…it would be too embarrassing for someone calling herself Ammo Grrrll to ask for help in cleaning guns.)

Four. I resolve to clean out and organize all my files. I'm pretty confident that I will locate the gun manuals in my files. After which I can clean the guns while standing at my custom-made gun-cleaning bench in the garage. So I will be fulfilling three of my Resolutions at once. Righteous! Maybe even while eating a carrot (see below).

Five. I resolve to eat more vegetables. So far, in gearing up for Veggie-Rama 2018, and thanks to my new Salad Shooter, a Hanukkah gift, I have consumed some Zuchini Bread and Carrot Cake. Good start!

Six. I resolve to drink more coffee. Article after article appears in print and on The Internet touting the benefits of drinking 4-6 cups of coffee a day. I typically consume 3 cups a day, but I believe I can easily double that and still sleep well over 2 hours a night.

Seven. I resolve to drink more alcohol. Again, we are getting tons of information about the huge benefits of "moderate" drinking, including, but not limited to, red wine. I plan to multitask, adding either Jameson or Bailey's to my six cups of coffee. This should help with the insomnia. And make me both alert and relaxed while driving. Winning!

Eight. I resolve to learn how to turn on our television, what a "firestick" is, and what to do with the other six remotes besides the one that I've been shown several dozen times turns on the TV. Failing that, I will just continue to read, write, and play Brahms, Mozart, Country, and hip "new" pop music like The Eagles on my ancient CD player. I have to be the lowest-tech human left on the planet. There is very little on television that would make it worth learning how to use the remotes. Besides, Mr. AG is almost always home. And the Paranoid Texan next door is a TV Wizard. Literally. Haha. I just like to misuse the word "literally" in case I ever meet Joe Biden who is very devoted to that word.

Nine. I resolve to buy an item of "makeup" and learn how to use it to see if it really does "make up" for any beauty deficiencies. I think I will start with something easy like lipstick or mascara. Why is it nigh unto impossible to put on mascara with one's mouth closed? Strange.

Ten. I resolve to gain 10 lbs. Since I have failed at every single weight-related resolution for the last 40 years, I am going to try to gain weight and see if I can be a failure at that.

Eleven. I resolve to eschew political discussion with anyone who hates President Trump. It is like trying to convince a mental patient who believes that he is Napoleon that he is not; it will not convince him and will only irritate him. Sometime you might need a good Napoleon to invade a country or come to a party, and you will be sorry you alienated him by kindly pointing out, say, 27 ways in which he is mistaken. Why is that kind of correction so infrequently appreciated by others when we all so love it ourselves?

Twelve. I resolve to be more patient and kind with my family and friends, to be more grateful for the countless blessings I enjoy. I consider this little blogging community to be an extended family, ready with words of encouragement, praise and friendly banter, though so far no one has offered a loan of a truly interesting amount. When you peruse other blogs' comments, you realize that even our trolls are quite civil. God bless us every one.

Continued bottomless gratitude to the PL boys for giving me this platform, and to my insanely loyal readers who make MY Fridays worth all that health-depriving sitting at my terminal. I will never blame you if I die 10 years prematurely because of it.

HAPPY NEW YEAR!! May it be one of peace, joy, good health and more winning. Suh-weet!!

JANUARY, FEBRUARY, MARCH

2018 kicks off with a bang and the novel idea that "credibly accused" is just as good as "innocent until proven guilty" in the New American Jurisprudence. No accusation is too old or too trivial or too unsubstantiated to count in order to destroy a man's professional or personal life. Could it ever blow up in the faces of the leftists who rely on it? Naaah. That's crazy talk.

Next up is a critical discussion of the disturbing trend of hotels to eliminate bathtubs and the several things that are wrong with showers. There is a column dubbed "Random Thoughts" that is exactly that, and then a nod to French/Spanish diarist, Anais Nin, and my pathetic attempts to journal.

There will be a nice soliloquy on the incredible abundance we have individually and collectively in this great and good land; a parody of the butt-covering emails various corrupt Obama Administration hacks sent to themselves, a discussion of why the unpopular platform planks of the leftists require a whole new set of voters, a personal rags to "modest prosperity" story, and more defense of our Second Amendment rights in the face of the Parkland school shooting disaster.

The final month of the March-to-March Ammo Grrrll Year kicks off with a pretty funny list of "12 Things More Accurate than CNN", a nostalgic look back at Daylight Savings Time, one more swipe at Hillary over her 300th whining explanation for why she lost the election. (Spoiler alert: not HER fault; stupid redneck Deplorable women!)

As all anniversary columns, we end with a celebration called "The Column Turns 4."

CREDIBLY ACCUSED

January 5, 2018

Maybe 20 or 25 years ago I recorded on VHS tape a comedy set by a very funny Southern comic named Blake Clark. He had one bit I particularly liked that I will paraphrase badly now: "A man goes into a bank to rob it. He is captured on security tape IN the bank. There are several witnesses IN the bank who can identify him. The teller has hit the silent alarm. The robber comes out of the bank and is arrested… WITH the gun and the loot. And in the evening's news report, the media calls him … 'the SUSPECT.'" Who, of course, has been advised by his lawyer to plead "Not Guilty."

This hypothetical bank robber caught in broad daylight with a mountain of evidence has far more rights than any man accused of sexual assault, sexual harassment, touching, or "making a woman 'uncomfortable'," itself apparently a brand new crime. Being "comfortable" is now a God-given legal right – evidently just for women — along with life, liberty and the pursuit of publicity. Who knew?

And how is a man described who has any of the above sex charges flung at him? CREDIBLY ACCUSED. What a charming new weasel phrase THAT is. "Credible" to whom?

When a stripper/hooker said she was raped at Duke, 88 faculty members found her word enough to demand the immediate expulsion of the "credibly accused" students plus – but, of course – a full scholarship offered to the drug-addled accuser.

When a delusional, lonely woman made up an imaginary lover who took her to a fraternity party and then organized her gang-rape, otherwise intelligent people – and a woman writer for Rolling Stone — found this laughably-unlikely scenario totally believable and the fraternity boys were "credibly accused." Ah, all women must be believed, right? Even the certifiable.

So ingrained now into our social justice culture is the verifiably false notion that all women are telling the truth about sex that vast sums of taxpayer monies have been paid out on behalf of politicians. How many were for dreadful acts and how many were just to "make things go away" we have no way of knowing. This is surely not to imply that a lot of those grotesque excuses for human beings are not, in fact, scum-sucking pigs. But, think for one New York minute about the potential for get-rich schemes by #Me-Too accusers.

To be accused is to be guilty without any forum for confronting your accuser, determining the facts, or even – in the case of Tavis Smiley and hundreds of college boys – finding out what you have been accused of! Franz Kafka, meet Joseph Stalin.

Here are several things I know about men, women, and sex: these aren't popular or permitted things to say, but they are true. Women like to be wanted, to be pursued, to flirt and try to seduce. To deny this reality is to be dishonest. Why else do you need a gas mask to get into an office building elevator filled with young secretaries? Who needs perfume to go to work?

The entire clothing industry is geared to be either peekaboo revealing or downright slutty. The sole purpose of a deep v-neck blouse is to say, "Woohoo, look at me. I have large breasts!" I defy anyone – of any gender – NOT to look when a woman is displaying six inches of cleavage. She can be disingenuous and point to her eyes and say, "I'm up here," but then, why the heck are you wearing that shirt, honey?? I'm not saying she should be ashamed; I'm just saying she should admit the effect she is after and own it.

When the actresses in Hollywood wear Oscar dresses with 2 ounces of fabric, when Megyn and Mika have publicity shots that could be accurately described as "vampy" at best, what is the message here? I will put up my Dream House in Arizona in a bet that no network of any kind will ever hire an on-camera "journalist" who looks like the late and unlamented Helen Thomas. Make no mistake; I do not want women in burqas. I just don't want them pretending that they aren't trading on their looks and sex appeal. They are. And then getting all huffy and demanding money when a man responds.

Men are hard-wired to respond. They will try, especially when they feel that there has been at least a hint of a shadow of a penumbra of an invitation to do so. This, kids, is how people become couples and how, eventually, new people come into the world!

Ben Affleck was accused of touching one woman's breast some 15-20 years ago. He has apologized and given the obligatory nod to how brave and important it is that these ancient accusations see the light of day. I am guessing that often alcohol is involved as well as "mixed messages" about whether such a touch would be welcome. Sometimes in these lurid tales it is reported that the woman told others at the time that it had happened. You bet your life she did! And there is an excellent chance that she dined out on it and hoped that it might mean that Ben would call her in the future. But now she will get more out of joining the vast, professional-victim horde of offended delicate maidens.

We have had several decades now of raunchy women proclaiming liberation from old-fashioned notions of ladylike behavior. A popular comedienne had an opening line: "My mother has a bumper sticker that says 'Honk if you've f——d my daughter.'" Recently, Mr. AG and I were watching a standup showcase with six new comedians. After a couple of pretty funny opening acts, a cute, young blonde woman did 10 graphic, gross, cringe-worthy, and unfunny minutes on the mechanics of anal sex. After 30 years in the trenches, I am pretty hard to shock, but Mr. AG and I just stared at each other in disbelief before turning it off.

We had Sex in the City, in which the women had much sex with many partners and then gathered to talk about sex and silly overpriced shoes. We had House of Cards, in which the now-disgraced Kevin Spacey playing a Democrat politician had sex with men and women and had some inconvenient partners killed afterwards. Our culture is marinated in porn-level sex 24/7 and yet men are supposed to behave at all times like blind monks.

"Credibly accused" is no substitute for "Innocent until proven guilty." Danger, Will Robinson! Giving power-mad, leftwing feminists the unassailable right to use unsubstantiated, decades-old accusations as a weapon in the War on Men is like giving razor blades to a chimp. Except that, to my knowledge, chimps don't deliberately lie for fame and profit.

SHOWERED WITH HATRED

January 12, 2018

I have been reluctant to take on today's subject for some time, so controversial is its nature. Viral shaming, death threats, rampant mockery may well follow. But inspired by the profligate flinging about of the word "brave" to describe every woman who has a lurid, decades-old tale of being touched once by another human being, I have decided to come clean.

Am I talking about abortion, sexual assault, or moving the US Embassy to Jerusalem? No. I am speaking, of course, of Bath People (me and all right-thinking Americans) vs. Shower People (Mr. AG, every man I know, and commies, Literal Nazis, and Harvey Weinstein).

Having traveled for 30 years for work — and still, after 8 years of retirement not yet completely out of tiny soap – it came as a great shock to me to check into a Marriott Courtyard to discover that my room had NO BATHTUB!!

I'm surprised it still had a toilet. Soon that will be gone to make room for more places to plug in chargers for electronics.

Evidently, people over 60 fear bathtubs and people younger than 60 have such a marked preference for showers that hotels have stopped even bothering to offer bathtubs.

The home I grew up in had only one bathroom for five people. My sister got the first 2 hours in the morning and the other 4 of us split the remaining 17 minutes. The bathroom had only a bathtub and no shower and I loved bathing from early childhood on. What Kramer on Seinfeld slanderously described as "marinating in your own filth."

The first time I ever ran a full tub was my first day at college. Sadly, our dear late Mama had grown up on a farm in drought-ridden South Dakota in the Depression. All water had to be hauled from a spring in cream cans. Her parents and sisters all bathed in the same metal tub on Saturday night. She hated "wasting" water (or anything else…) When we were kids, she allowed us about two inches of water, and, since the bathroom wall abutted the kitchen wall, she could hear if we tried to sneak more water and would bang on the wall, bless her heart. I would bathe in one inch of water for life if I could have her back for one week…

But it's not like I have never seen a shower. I saw one in the Hitchcock movie Psycho, and it made a definite and lasting impression on me.

Our home in Arizona has three full bathrooms and one half-bath off the living room area for guests who have only come to eat, drink and be merry, and have courteously attended to their hygiene needs before arriving. So we have three showers and three bathtubs.

The bathtub in the Master Bath is a very deep, short, kind of wide-oval affair that Mr. AG once referred to as "a Susan-shaped tub" and yet he still lives and breathes, though slightly less well. Anyway, one can run a lovely hot bath, submerge every part in it up to one's neck, and float in an Epsom-salt sea of tranquility. When the skin on one's fingers resembles Craisins only not quite as red, one can run the washcloth briefly around the "ring" and then hustle right out into a big, soft, warmed towel or terrycloth robe.

Showers? A totally different experience. I happen to have very dry hair, so I only wash my hair once or twice a week, and when I wash my hair, I do it in the big walk-in shower in the master bath. And hate, hate, hate every minute of it.

Here are just a few of the downsides of a shower:

Even in Arizona, on a 38 degree morning (66 inside, and not yet meeting Mr. AG's rigorous standards for paying for heat), whichever side is in the shower spray, the other side is freezing cold.

In the hot summer, when the AC fan is on, a stiff North Wind is blowing on your wet, naked body. I hope the words "stiff," "wet," and "naked" in one sentence do not violate the sensible new Taste Standards. In no way do I attribute these qualities to the GOPe or even acknowledge that there is such a thing.

When a random husband hypothetically flushes the toilet in another room, the temperature in the shower can drop from "pleasant" to "prohibited by the Geneva Convention" in a nanosecond.

When rinsing off facing the spray, leaving your eyes wide open is painful, but closing them leaves you vulnerable to Norman Bates.

Finally, and worse even than Norman Bates, which at least would be mercifully quick, there is a chance that Harvey Weinstein could appear and demand that you watch him shower. I think he may still be in Arizona. To my knowledge, so far no Hollywood perv has insisted that a woman watch him bathe. Because civilized, patriotic Americans bathe, obviously. That, and the water is too deep to see much of interest.

When you are finished with your shower, and turn OFF the hot water, you now must spend several moist and chilly minutes cleaning up by imitating a professional beggar with a squeegee, scraping down the shower sides and door. (Where are the Squeegee People when they could be useful?)

I invite rebuttal comments from The Shower People, who vastly outnumber us Bathers. You will all be mistaken, but that's how fair and balanced we at Power Line are.

Stay tuned in future weeks for: Toilet Paper Roll Etiquette: over the top or coming from under? We report, you decide.

PETITIONING FOR A FRIEND

January 19, 2018

Of all the things I hate to do – flying, going to the doctor every five to seven years for my annual check-up, being assaulted by CNN in airports (See: Flying) – approaching strangers to get them to sign a petition has to be very high on my list. And yet that is what I have been doing for several weeks on behalf of a good friend, Glenn Morrison, who is running for Constable of Pinal County here in Arizona. Up until Glenn threw his hat in the ring, I had no idea that we HAD a Constable or even what a Constable did. I assumed it maybe had something to do with housing horses. That is incorrect. Look it up.

We needed around 300 signatures to qualify for ballot status. In truth, we "need" fewer than that, but PEOPLE LIE and say that they are Republicans, when in fact, they are Democrats. This is not surprising – I would be ashamed to say I was a Democrat, too, but it turns out that it is not embarrassment that drives them, but deliberate deception.

Since Glenn is running in the Republican primary and we ask specifically if people are Independents or Republicans before they can sign, some people are so disrespectful of the process that they would deliberately misrepresent their voter registration status in order to invalidate the signatures and render all your work for naught.

Going house to house in my own neighborhood was a joy and a chance to get to know a few more of my neighbors. Almost my whole long block – both sides – is solid Republican. Even the few Democrats I ran into outside our Village Clubhouse were perfectly polite, with a couple of rare rude exceptions from New York and Boston. (No! Surely not!)

Seeking signatures in the Greater DLV outside our subdivision is complicated by the fact that we have so many snowbirds and Canadians cluttering up our Malls and invigorating our economy. If you are not a Resident of Pinal County, you cannot vote here or sign a petition. Though, clearly, many non-citizens from various poopy-pants countries* vote anyway.

Anyhow, here are a few of my observations of the petitioning experience, once I MADE MYSELF get out of the house and actually do the work:

Almost every single flippin' person is on their flippin' phone – and no, NOT a "flip" phone. What is the matter with people who are texting while walking across Walmart's busy parking lot with cars going every direction? They can't ALL be waiting on a kidney transplant! I will say this – a phone makes a great natural barrier between you and a potential solicitor. People HATE being approached by anyone unless they are handing out free stuff. If they see you with a clipboard in hand, they will walk to a whole different Walmart door to avoid eye contact.

Even if they give you a wide berth, however, IF you are nimble, relentless and able to block their path, once you do your pitch, about half of them will say, "Not interested," "NO" or "I don't know enough about that to sign." But, the other half will go along with you if you are smiling and friendly and holding a .45 with no obvious safety. Haha. I kid again.

Many of our fellow citizens are AFRAID to sign anything, afraid to be on "some list." When you look at the Stalinism at Google, the Lois Lerners at the IRS, this is sad, but not irrational. Two men said that they would love to sign but were convicted felons. Oh, well. Try Minnesota!

I found that when I explained that Glenn was running in the

Republican primary and you had to be "either an Independent or a Republican" to sign, and made it clear that I did not need to know which, the vast majority of people who agreed to sign were EAGER to assure me they were a Republican. Which I hope bodes well for 2018.

Way more men were willing to sign than women, maybe because of my petitioning outfit of Daisy Duke short shorts, a tube top, fishnet stockings and high heels. Because nothing looks cuter on a woman over 70 than that outfit. No, but seriously my friends, women either said they were Democrats, or did not wish to be on a list, or avoided me altogether. Women WITH men signed in equal numbers with the men. It was always so great to get a "two-fer."

Let me tell you a little about Glenn. He is a Constitutional Republican. He is my shooting instructor, and also instructs LEOs; he is quite simply, the best teacher of ANYTHING I have ever had. He rides with the Sheriff's Posse protecting the border. He also rides with a motorcycle drill team. He's a great cook. And the kind of friend you would want in a fight.

One small personal anecdote about him before I ask for a little support. A few years back, when I knew him only as my husband's instructor, Mr. AG was on an extended trip to Israel. My closest friends are Minnesota snowbirds who had not yet arrived. It was a very lonely time, my mother was sick and I had one of those "close-to-rock-bottom" afternoons. I called Glenn to see if he could get coffee or see a movie. Something. Anything. He said he was in Tucson. I thought that was the end of it. Several hours later, he called and said he was back in town and thought I had sounded "down" and he was concerned about me. I practically sprinted over to play with his great Beagle, Jasmine, and watch TV with him and his wife. It would be overdramatic to say it saved my life, but it sure did lift my spirits.

Also, if he had not taught me to shoot, this column would not exist. Can you regulars even bear to contemplate the bleak emptiness of your Friday mornings? Oh, the humanity!

Even a little local race is ridiculously expensive. Glenn had hoped to raise just $5,000. His opponent has a "money is no object" attitude. Glenn is not wealthy, just committed. He doesn't need the same level of donations as a person facing an illness or accident. Heck, donations in the $20-50 range would be awesome. $20 buys a lawn sign. (That's two lattes and a scone!) Do it for a good guy who is a friend of YOUR friend, Ammo Grrrll, who works her fingers to the bone every week for free in order to entertain you! I thank you in advance from the bottom of my heart. Glenn can be found at MorrisonforConstable.com.

*In deference to the delicate sensibilities of Democrats who use the adorable phrase "c*ck-holster," giggle at bloody, severed heads, and think "F*ck Trump" projected on a football stadium is high humor, I am using the tasteful "poopy-pants" instead of the more vulgar "sh*thole countries," whether or not the President said it.

RANDOM *THOUGHTS IN SEARCH OF A TOPIC*

January 26, 2018,

A topic, a topic, my kingdom for a topic. Writing a weekly column in which one is expected to be accurate, interesting, and intentionally rather than inadvertently humorous is a particular kind of challenge. Oh, sure, anybody can make her readers laugh by stupidly typing ".9" for "9 mm" caliber ammo in a column in which said hypothetical writer purports to know SOMETHING about guns 'n ammo. That was my most embarrassing moment so far, but I'm confident I will top it one day. To my everlasting distress, I continue to be relentlessly human.

The rub with a weekly column comes in the same way that it comes for housewives to whom falls all the cooking in the household. Mama and I would frequently discuss the daily grind of coming up with ideas for "what's for dinner?" – although we called it "supper" in rural Minnesota — and also our occasional desire to lay a cast iron skillet upside the head of the next person who asked us that question. (Old standbys in a pinch: Waffles; Grilled Cheese/Tomato Soup; Chicken Pot Pies; or Chipped Beef on Chow Mein Noodles.)

It wasn't so much the cooking itself, we agreed, as the onus of coming up with IDEAS for what to cook. I mean, really, how much trouble is it to stick a few baking potatoes into the oven along with a roasting hen? Or throw a few steaks on the grill? Open a can of corn or simmer a few frozen peas and call it dinner. Keep bringing out little containers of things like pickles (dill and sweet), olives, some iffy coleslaw that has already been rejected three times, and assorted condiments to make the table look less pathetic.

Once, in a galaxy far, far away (OK, New York City), I worked in an anti-war office. In fact, I was part of a staff of about 40 largely unemployable, lazy, young radicals. This is why I laughed out loud when Barack Hussein Obama described himself as a "community organizer." I had known these people; I had BEEN these people, and I knew what a bunch of useless slugs they (we) were.

The 26-year-old who supervised us was once tasked with composing a fund-raising letter to be sent out to the wealthier liberal suckers who financed us "kids" doing the grunt work. For days, every time I went by his desk, he appeared to be hard at work on this singular task, scowling into a yellow legal pad. On the day the letter was to have been typed, mimeographed, and sent out in a bulk mailing, he finally showed me what he had so far.

He had only the salutation, which read "Dear Monkey Meat."

It was not my first inkling that he and several other of my co-workers might be clinically insane. Now I empathize with his writer's block. So we have established that the first problem with writing, especially after 200-ish columns, is coming up with a TOPIC. Once I have a topic or a taking off point, I can write like the wind. In fact, I am known as a very windy writer.

The other major problem, which you have heard me whine about before, is that with writing just once a week, if a juicy thing happens on Thursday, when I have already submitted my Friday column the day before, it will be 8 long days before I can comment amusingly upon it. In Blog World, eight days might as well be a decade. All the humor has been wrung out of it by the hundreds of bloggers and commenters alike. Damn not only my 4 esteemed witty colleagues, but our clever commenters, who are frequently more pithy than us bloggers. After eight days, pith is in short supply.

A case in point: I had nearly finished a guaranteed Pulitzer-contending column discussing the shocking fact that the Democrats preferred to screw U.S. citizens, including the military, in order to keep the illegal alien DREAMERS here. Fed, educated, incarcerated, and medicated for free by taxpayers. Then Trump illustrated the obvious in the way only he dared to and the whole Resistance Lite collapsed like Hillary being heaved into a waiting van. The cowardly virtue-signalers must have circulated their internal polling data and by last Monday already decided to run for cover. Column status: Dead On Arrival. Ammo Grrrll hardest hit! Pulitzer Dreamer's hopes evaporating like sweat in Arizona in August.

I had a hilarious column in its embryonic stages before that on the flimsy life raft the Democrats cling to that Trump is crazy and unfit for office. ("You there – the one in the vagina costume barking at the moon – what was your question again about sanity?") But the handsome Presidential Doctor faced the bleating little sheeple of the White House Press Corps and put our minds at ease over the questions that keep us all awake at night — like whether or not our President wears dentures. He does not. Whew! Good to know.

The great songwriter, John Prine – whom I have opened for! – has a lyric, channeling a weary, jaded middle-aged guy that goes, "I'm sitting on the front steps drinking Orange Crush, wondering if it's possible if I could still blush." Embarrassment is a vital human emotion. Do these miserable little trained seals ever DVR one of the press conferences and cringe when they see themselves ask for the 22nd time if the physician is SURE that he didn't miss that critical "tell" of Presidential Insanity that would allow impeachment to go forward? I guess you would need a modicum of self-awareness for that. Asked and answered.

And so, in the end, with two columns kaput, I will just write about American Generosity. Last week, some 133 people, most complete strangers, contributed $6,249 to my candidate for Constable, Glenn Morrison. Money they could just as well have used for a nice evening out, a fine bottle of Scotch, or a toy for a grandkid. Think about that for a minute. What a country!! Since I was the one who asked for your support, it is only fitting that I am the one to express my profound gratitude. But I want to end with Glenn's own words:

The generous outpouring of support from Ammo Grrrll's friends and fans is stunning! The concerns over how to fund such an important campaign have been weighing heavily on me and huge load has been lifted. The people I am working to serve deserve the best possible person for the job, not just the person who can spend the most. I now stand at least a fighting chance!! For the first in a couple of months, I'm to be able to sleep tonight. From the bottom of the heart, I thank you all for your support.

A DIARIST FOR THE AGES

February 2, 2018

Many years ago, I bought a six-volume set of the Diaries of Anais Nin, a famous Spanish-Cuban-French woman who chronicled every waking minute of her life in diaries. It inspired me to give it a go. Almost immediately, it became clear that she was living a much more exciting life than mine and that I was about to turn out the most boring and repetitive diary in the history of that, or any, literature.

Anais Nin (who is often a crossword puzzle answer now since "Anais" has so many vowels) wrote about having cocktails and deep conversations with Henry Miller and Gertrude Stein in Paris. She knew everyone who was anyone. She also – and I mean no "slut-shaming" judgment here – apparently had sex with everyone with a pulse on several continents. My diary quickly lapsed into grocery lists, recipes, restaurant meals I loved, and – here's a shock! – diet failures.

Even when I traveled to more interesting places than suburban St. Paul, Minnesota, the journal could have been marketed as a sleep aid: "Maui is really pretty. The people here are so nice. Why did I order Macadamia Nut Pie for dessert again? At breakfast. When I get back home, I really have to try that low-carb thing again."

"Israel is really pretty. Also very historic. The people here speak Hebrew which I do not. There is only so far one can get with just the Torah blessing as conversation. The food is awesome, especially the Israeli Breakfast Buffet. I love the fresh-squeezed orange juice and the falafel stands, too. When we get home, I plan to try a juice fast."

"Amsterdam is really pretty. The people are big and tall and blonde, like Minnesotans. They get Argentine beef here, which is really tender. I do not know why so many Dutch women sit in windows with most of their clothes off – what's up with that? I plan to try the Smoothie Diet when I get home. And then maybe sit in a bay window in my flannel nightie. Memo to self: discuss with Mr. AG if we should put in a bay window."

Since the diary idea – called "journaling" in Lady Speak now – was such a bust, I am sticking to my strength, which is "list making." Every single day since 7th grade, I have made a To Do List and checked off every item. If I do something NOT on the list, I PUT it on the list. And then I check it off. It is important to me to feel like I am accomplishing something. Especially in retirement, when I consider it an accomplishment to know what day of the week it is.

Mr. AG once told me that Revolutionary Hero and 2nd President, John Adams, was an inveterate daily To Do list maker. Although, while my list has items like "Drink 3 cups coffee"; "Floss twice"; "Meditate for 10 Minutes"; "Iron 4 pillowcases"; "Think About Column"; "Maybe Start Writing Column"; and "Go to the Post Office", John Adams' To Do List was rather weightier:

"Contact Thom Jefferson as Writing Partner"
"Draft Declaration of Independence" with TJ
"Join 90 Revolutionary Committees, Chair 25" (Seriously)
"Brief Nap"
"Agree to be General Washington's VP"
Become known as "The Father of the Navy"
Run for President after George

And so on…

I have a t-shirt I bought during the Obama Ammo Drought

Era at a gun show, using the famous "gunshow t-shirt exception" that allows you a free t-shirt with every fully-auto Uzi and sawed-off shotgun you buy with no background check. Just ask the Babbling Bimbo Gun Experts (of either gender) in The Media how easy that is. I wear that shirt a lot less since I got holes in it from bore cleaning fluid. But here is the message I was drawn to:

"AMERICA: Designed by Geniuses; Run by Idiots."

We stand on shoulders so tall we could never be grateful enough. Yes, the World War II Generation was a Great Generation to be sure. They fought and died to preserve and protect the land and liberty they had inherited as a birthright and saved the world from fascism. But those patriots in the 1700s fashioned this Republic from whole cloth with no blueprint – the mind reels! What a crime that the anti-American left-wing lunatics in charge of educating our young people for several decades now will soon not teach the history! of these intellectual giants at all. Icky Old White Men! Who never said a word about men in dresses being able to potty amidst the actual ladies and girls!

And yet not a one of those NFL millionaire kneelers or howling harridans with their obscene signs and pink hats can point to a better system, a country with more opportunity for every single grievance group they represent. And if they can, why don't they move there?

If I believed that the United States were as anti-Semitic as the BLM people claim it is racist, I would move to Israel before I even finished this column.

The professional Grievance Grubbers promise every election to leave if their candidate loses and they never do. Liars and welshers as well as idiots. The countries they cite as Paradise have to erect barbed wire and high walls with gun turrets – Cuba, Venezuela, the former Soviet Union, North Korea, East Germany — to keep their delighted citizens IN. And we have to – please, God – have some sort of a wall to keep invaders out, since our reputation as Racist, Sexist Deplorables is not, evidently, enough to deter them.

It's almost as if they know it isn't true!

UNNECESSARY ABUNDANCE

February 9, 2018

My beautiful daughter-in-law sent us several thoughtful gifts for Chanukah or Mr. AG's birthday or just because she is generous and Amazon Prime-addicted. Whatever.

One of the gifts is a spectacular set of steak knives. She probably noticed at last visit that I had just set out paring knives for our steaks. She is an excellent cook, daughter of a professional chef, and I'm sure this was a culinary faux pas of the highest order, but she was too kind to mention it. She is as kind as she is smart and beautiful. Good job, son!

Because she can see that my entire house was painted and decorated by my Mexican handyman, and features a riot of gaudy colors, each steak knife has a different colored handle. They are perfect in every way, including the number. Eight.

The Paranoid Texan Next Door has a slotted knife repository the size of a small ottoman on his counter that has 12 steak knives. Trust me, if I ever have 12 people for a meal, steak will not be on the menu! That is a Chili or Lasagna Party if ever I heard of one. But, needless to say, the collection does not end with just steak knives. Oh, no.

The PT once pointed out the name of every knife – The Chef's Knife, the Bread Knife, the Bobbitt Bobber, the Bass De-Gutter, the Meat Tenderizer Mallet, The Tofu Pulverizer, The Boning Knife, The Squirrel Skinner, The Cheese Knife, The Football Deflator, the set of 12 never-even-once-used

Grapefruit Knives, the Blind Mice Tail-Carving Knife, The Mushroom Mincer, the Getting Stuck Toast Out of the Toaster Knife (with Optional Defibrillator), and the Bowie Knife. There were many more, but even though I was wearing sunglasses, eventually he noticed I had nodded off over post-walk coffee at his breakfast bar. (Mr. AG is a runner, so I walk with the PT. I do not run. Not even for a bus.)

When I woke up, I asked him how many of these knives he had ever used and he said, he was pretty sure at least 3, but one of those was The Scissors. And I thought about how many gadgets, how much task-specific crap we own and never, ever use. Mango Dicer, anyone?

Oh, don't get me wrong – I LOVE gadgets and I love American ingenuity and clever inventors and the dozens of aisles of "fun" things you cannot do without at Bed Bath and Beyond. But even in The Arizona Dream Kitchen, with 26 cupboards and 7 large drawers, I am plumb out of space to store frivolous utensils. Hard-boiled egg slicer? Avocado Cutter?

It is instructive to remember my early years when our motto was Make Do. I cut shortening into flour for pie crust with two table knives. Now I have a pastry blender that is always getting stuck sideways in the drawer, and which can only be remedied by violently shaking the drawer and swearing. The swearing seems to be a critical element of the process. As a young bride, I cut biscuits out of the dough with an upside down drinking glass. Now I have biscuit cutters in several sizes. And mostly use Pillsbury biscuits anyway, which have improved so much over the years as to make homemade barely worth the trouble.

Put down your coffee cup, my friend, and survey your surroundings. Can you even BELIEVE how much STUFF you have? My parents lived very modestly in the 1500 sq. ft. home I grew up in. But we didn't realize how much stuff there was – in the basement, attic, garage — to "down-size" when we moved them from their home to a spacious Assisted Living unit. Then, when Mama needed more care after a bad fall, we moved them to a smaller 2-room suite in a different facility and down-sized once more. Finally, after Mama passed, "we" – and by "we" I mean my brother and his sainted wife — moved Daddy to a yet smaller single room. And Daddy STILL has a lot of stuff he will never use or wear.

I am using the Royal We here. My sister and I got in on one move each; our brother lucked into all three. That's what you get for being kind, strong as an ox, and having some helpful children and a pickup. My main contribution was to have great friends who still live in my hometown. Thanks again, Bonnie and Wayne!

Unless the person is a junkie who has sold everything he owns to buy drugs, almost every person in America has more possessions than wealthy people a few generations ago. In my family, we are just one generation away from outdoor privies which my mother grew up with. Daddy's family did have indoor plumbing – one bathroom for 2 adults and 6 children under 10.

Even in a regular old supermarket – not Byerly's, AJs or whatever your upscale market is – the choices, the variety, the astonishing array of fresh produce and exotic fruits should take our breath away, but we take it for granted. We eat better than the Kings of Europe back in the day, potentates who never tasted a banana or pineapple or Salted Caramel Gelato.

All this awesome abundance has been brought to us by American capitalism, ingenuity and enterprise. And still there are millions of young people who think Bernie Sanders' "one deodorant" program is the way to go. (Possibly because leftists don't use deodorant.) Shared scarcity sounds so much better on paper. Speaking of paper, what are the chances that Sheryl Crow uses only the one square of toilet tissue she advocates to save the planet?

If people voluntarily want to simplify a la Thoreau, have at it. When we sold our home in Minnesota to move permanently to Arizona, we had to make some tough choices, especially with our thousands of books. Every once in a while, I think of an item that didn't make the cut and wish I had it – where IS that nice salad bowl I got at my wedding shower? — but the feeling passes pretty quickly. I hope some Goodwill shopper is using it with joy, and finally finding the arugula the Obamas wanted the poor to have. And I remind myself that I have five other salad bowls. None of which has seen a leaf of arugula, which always sounds to me like some sort of unfortunate sexually-transmitted disease. Just sayin'.

So, I will finish this meditation on Abundance and Gratitude in a minute and turn to thinking Deep Thoughts about the Deep State or the FBI or who in my neighborhood besides the woman with the suspicious "Bears" banner is probably a Russian Bot. Right after I wash my three Deviled Egg Plates and Asparagus Platter. I mean, really, who could pass up a little platter with the imprint of asparagus in it? Have you no soul? Have you no VISA?

EMAIL TO SELF

February 15, 2018

To: Ammogrrrll
From: Ammogrrrll
Cc: Mr. AG
In re: Missing Key Lime Pie

It has come to my attention that the remainder of the Key Lime Pie (nearly ¾ of the pie, as it happens) appears to be missing. In no way could this have been consumed by me and certainly not in one sitting while Mr. AG was at the dentist.

I know this did not happen because I was specifically told by my doctor that my cholesterol has been creeping up from "ridiculously-high" to "sludge-level." And since I was told not to do things like this, and always to follow the proper procedure for storage of Pie, Key Lime, it did not happen.

Thank God I have this record proving that I did not do anything inappropriate with the Key Lime Pie or with the Double Chocolate Fudge Brownies either, which I am confident are still safely in the freezer right next to where the Lemon Bars used to be. I always store Fudge Brownies the proper way, what we here in Protect Thine Patootie Land call "by the book." Or, in this instance, by the Lemon Bars. Well, technically, where they used to be. Or would be, were they not also gone missing. Some kind of Baked Goods Bermuda Triangle is my best guess.

To: Ammogrrrll
From: Ammogrrrll
In re: 2017 Tax Return

I sure am glad that I, in no way, have ever made a mistake in regards to legal deductions as defined by TurboTax. When TurboTax speaks, I listen, Boy Howdy. Always go by the book, says TurboTax, and that suits me right down to the ground.

Sometimes there are grey areas not entirely covered by TurboTax, such as what constitutes "a separate office." Does there have to be a desk, for example? When is a queen-size guest bed a perfectly-appropriate work space? And why have file cabinets in a "paperless" office? When you can have a little mini-fridge instead.

What a lucky break that I happen to have this unimpeachable record from myself to myself promising that I did not violate the spirit of the law, as defined by TurboTax. I am known as a very spiritual person. Oh wait, that was Donna Brazile who did not give Hillary any debate questions in advance because Donna stated emphatically that she is a black woman and a very spiritual Christian to boot, which is all well and good, but apparently, she failed to send herself an email saying she did not do that, and therefore was fired. If only a nice exculpatory email from herself to herself had been found she would not have had to write that book about how Hillary stole the nomination from Bernie that just needlessly upset so many people.

But back to the little tax issue and the quibbling over what constitutes a separate office. I am also attaching a picture of the "office" which may look like a guestroom, especially with the guests in it, but which I can assure you is an office. And a separate one at that, so separate that it looks exactly like a guest casita. But it is not. Because I say it is not. In this email.

To: Ammogrrrll
From: Ammogrrrll

In re: Weight Watcher weigh-in

Good Heavens! Weight Watchers must be using that broken scale again! It is not possible that I have gained 7 lbs. in just a week. I know this to be a fact because Weight Watchers has told me to stick to the program – by the book! – and I have. In fact, WW specifically mentions avoiding Key Lime Pie, Double Chocolate Fudge Brownies and Lemon Bars, so those things in particular I did not eat. Because my WW coach said "Do not do this." And so I didn't.

Someone might think that I had done that anyway, but then I can show them this email and they will be convinced that I had not done anything wrong. It is always good to make a thorough record of things you absolutely did not do.

Think what needless anguish poor Harvey Weinstein has gone through because he failed to email himself assuring the public that he never asked women to watch him shower because, for the love of Pete, WHO would DO that??

But back to Weight Watchers. Not that I am going back. When they refuse to use my own scale or even allow me to weigh in naked. It is possible I may have made a math error computing the number of "points" I am allowed on the program. I used to have a sexist Barbie Doll that said, "Math is hard," so I just flat-out gave up. So that must explain the discrepancy between LOSING 2 pounds and gaining 7. Because I did nothing wrong, as any fool can see by this email.

RECRUITING NEW DEMOCRATS

February 16, 2018

The summer of my junior year of high school, my boyfriend arranged for us to see The Smothers Brothers at the Grandstand Show at the Minnesota State Fair. They were an absolute delight – clean, fresh, hilarious – and became one of my earliest influences.

Little did I know then, of course, that I would open for the Smothers Brothers at a private event for the Minnesota Grocers Association a mere quarter century later. Dick and Tommy were extremely kind, encouraging, and gentlemanly toward me, a relatively new comic, and appeared to be very nice people.

But here's my actual point: their act was exactly the same as it had been when I saw them in 1963. Word for word. I knew because I had memorized it. It was a timeless, highly-professional act, and people loved it. They had no need to change it, because it wasn't "broke."

In the comedy business, unless you get a sitcom, there are really only two ways to make a living. You can have the insane work ethic of a Jerry Seinfeld and write new material for eight hours a day. However, with the exception of Jerry and a handful of others, most comics do not go into comedy to work hard. No. Had we wanted to work hard, we would have gone into mining, farming, trucking, construction, ranching, or air conditioning repair in Arizona. We like to say, "I love comedy. The pay is good, but the hour is great." How many people work for an hour a day, and get applause both before and after they show up for "work"?

But if you are not interested in putting your butt in a cheap desk chair and writing new material all day, you have one other option: You can perfect an act that really works and you can tour. Or, as we put it, "It's a lot easier to get a new audience than new material."

It turns out this is also true for political parties.

The Democrat Party has lurched so far left that it has alienated yuge swaths of the electorate. It is peddling the same stale, tired, hateful, divisive, grievance-grubbing "material" with the same ancient pitch-coots and spokes-crones. They desperately need a "new audience" of voters to replace the white working class and tax-paying middle classes of all colors whom they have gratuitously insulted and driven away. They are counting on voters who are young, stupid and influenced by endorsements from brain-dead celebrities. Sadly, these people frequently do not bother to vote, like Colin "Cops R Pigs Socks" Kaepernick. But more importantly, they need people who don't understand English with the exception of two words: "free stuff."

And hence the Democrats' fanatic death-grip commitment to open borders, sanctuary cities, chain migration and visa roulette. They must cling to these unpopular positions like barnacles clinging to a sinking ship because they have nothing else to offer. Not a thing. Here's a recap of just a few of the greatest hits of the Obama Era and continuing with the mighty P. Hat Resistance:

Like your doctor? You can't keep her. Haha. We were lying and laughing at you while we lied.

Hard-working, well-paid miner? We're going to kill coal. We don't even try to pretend otherwise; we are proud enough to say it outloud.

Are you an Asian-American who studied every spare minute of high school? You don't count. You need 400 more points on your college entrance exams than slackers of color in order to get into our prestigious schools. Sorry, Asians, your skin is not the right color. Well, it's not about color per se because many East Indians are darker than African-Americans, but Indians don't count either. Like Asians, Indians also engage in totally unfair studying, plus they have parents who read to them and go to parent-teacher conferences, that sort of privileged White Supremacy thing.

We are going to penalize, sue, and boycott any state that makes any effort to enforce national immigration laws. Same for hillbilly states that think women and girls should potty in their own bathrooms, free from the intrusion and danger of men in dresses.

We are going to call all women "brave" who claim to have had unwanted sexual contact just because they were accidentally drunk and naked in a man's apartment on the first date. Don't feel like making a fuss right now? Heck, you can wait years, decades even, to make scurrilous but brave charges it will be impossible to defend against. Put Gloria Allred on speed-dial and, in the unlikely event that it's possible for a zombie to pass away, her daughter will be right there to pick up the slack.

Anyway, back to the awesome planks in the Democrat platform. Think abortion is vile any time, but especially after the baby can feel pain and is viable? Tough noogies! Think the black family would be better off with jobs? You are hopeless racists! Black unemployment lowest in history is a BAD thing and the CBC won't STAND for it. Literally. But nothing is as bad as everything white. White people are privileged and evil. Every. Last. One. Ask Obama about his Grandma. Ask him while you're at it about his portrait "artist," a proud graduate of the Art School advertised on Matchbook Covers, whose main oeuvre is black people holding the decapitated heads of white people. Isn't that just adorable? Undoubtedly "brave," too.

Oh, and just in case you weren't turned off enough, we Democrats love disrespect to the flag and the Anthem. We hate guns unless they are held by our private security guards. We hate free speech on campus or in the workplace, but love kneeling during the National Anthem. That Free Speech is groovy.

Wow! With a platform this catchy and attractive, why in the world would the Democrats need to import 30 million indebted new voters and distribute them around the Red States? Got me.

A TREET FOR YOU

February 23, 2018

One of the more depressing things said by Nancy Pelosi, former Babbler of the House, was the notion that a $1,000 bonus is "crumbs." Almost nothing in the last ten years has been more symbolic of the divide in this country between the elite and the regular people that Kurt Schlichter, Townhall columnist par excellence, calls The Normals.

Since Nanny-State Nan declares that $1,000 is such a teensy, insignificant amount, what say we all just deduct $1,000 from what we owe the government on April 15th? Plus, we get to say what program we would like it deducted from. I would like half of mine taken out of the coffers of Planned Parenthood and the other half from the National Endowment for the Arts, Bullwhip up the Wazoo Division. How 'bout you? Just crumbs…nobody will miss them.

It has been a long time since $1,000 was our entire life savings, but I STILL think that a grand is a nice chunk of change. However, as I have discussed a few times before, there was a substantial period when an infusion of that kind of "crumb" would have been life-altering.

Jeff Foxworthy has made a lucrative and memorable career mining the inexhaustible lode of "You might be a redneck, if…" I enjoy his work very much and he seems like a terrific guy to boot. In homage, I will "borrow" a version of that formulation.

You might be really poor if…you buy a SPAM knock-off

called "Treet" because it was 4 cents cheaper than SPAM. Yeah, SPAM just wasn't wretched enough. Obviously, this was long before we started keeping imperfect kosher. This was in the first few months of our marriage when Mr. AG was still in college and I was taking home $167.50 every two weeks from my secretarial job. Budget, THAT, Nancy, I double-dog dare ya!

Truth to tell, though I would love for you to feel sorry for me, it wasn't even all that hard. Rent on our 2-room walk-up (5 floors) in Evanston was $115.00. If the place hasn't been torn down, the unit probably goes for $2500 a month now. You might be really poor if…you don't have a car. We didn't have a car; we walked or took the bus or El. In fact, we didn't have a car for the first seven years of our marriage!

You might be really poor if…you don't have a phone! Yes, it's true. We didn't have a phone. Well, we HAD a phone, but I was so lonesome for my dear Mama, and such a clueless bride, that I called too often and ran up – are you sitting down? — a $75.00 bill!

"Mama, my rye bread didn't rise! Is it too late to put in more yeast? Yeah, that's what I thought. Now I know how the Hebrews felt when they left Egypt. Welcome to Rye Matzo."

"Mama, the Meat Loaf all fell apart when I cut into it. Can I mash it up and make it into goulash with some tomatoes and macaroni?"

"Mama, (Mr. AG) says he's tired of Apple Pie and Chocolate Cake for dessert. How do you make that refrigerator dessert with the marshmallow fluff, graham cracker crust and canned cherry pie filling? OK, Ok, AND 3 cups of powdered sugar? Really? Boy, that sounds like a lot of sugar. I seem to be gaining weight and can't figure out why."

And so on. A very young bride needs her mother. But I could not rein in my dialing, so OUT came the phone. Which really left only rent, food, and utilities. My food budget was $25.00 a week and we ate very well. I planned two "budget" suppers a week – mac and cheese, liver and onions, tuna casserole, scrambled eggs – and the rest of the time we had Porterhouse steaks and Beef Roast or Fried Chicken, and all manner of fresh fruit and vegetables. I made all my desserts and bread from scratch. Usually with better results than the Rye Disaster.

That $25.00 bought four or five large bags of groceries which we schlepped home on foot, sometimes leap-frogging, setting one heavy bag down, moving the other one 50 feet ahead, then going back for the other one until we got home to the 5 flights of rickety stairs. God Bless the person who finally came up with handle bags!

What in heaven's name do young poor people – especially with children – do now for food?

I couldn't honestly tell you any more what I spend per week on food. Even if we didn't eschew pork, we are long past having to rely on Treet. I throw whatever I feel like into the market basket without regard to price. Every once in awhile I do look at the price of something and cannot believe it. Nearly $5.00 for our favorite loaf of bread? Seriously? When did that happen? Over $100 for filet mignon for six? Just "Choice" and not even "Prime." Even though I am sure there is massive cheating on the Food Stamp program, it's tough to begrudge the needy access to decent food, especially the working poor.

But back to 1967. You might be really poor if…you buy a hideous margarine called EAT-MOR which sold for 19 cents a pound. At least it seemed a step up from my mother's cost-cutting white margarine which came in a plastic bag with a dollop of orange dye in the middle. It was my job to pummel the bag until the dye turned the greasy goo a neon yellow. Lord only knows what the stuff was – probably Vaseline. Ultimately, even my tighter-than-elm-bark Mama returned to the wonderful butter of her youth on the farm.

We probably could have found a way to afford real butter in our $25/week budget, but all the doctors and health experts of that era promised us that margarine was much healthier than butter! Of course, we now know that the trans fats in margarine are among the worst things you can do to your body. We weren't supposed to eat eggs either. This made me forever skeptical of the pronouncements of "experts," whether on health matters or global warming.

I am hoping that in 20 years, we will learn that doughnuts are the perfect food to eat for long, healthy life. Raised glazed or the kind with Maple Frosting and crushed pistachios I get at one of my favorite restaurants in Phoenix: Chicken and Doughnuts. Of course, if I live 20 more years, I WILL have lived a long life, and arguably, already have. And, as I've said before, that's when I intend to take up smoking again, hard liquor and eating whatever I please. I figure the smoking will keep my weight down and, if not, the bourbon will make me not care.

BACK ATCHA!!

March 2, 2018

Because so few of the Professional Hysterics at CNN, the New York Times, or Democrat Shriek-Fests have ever actually fired a gun, they do not understand the very important concept of "ricochet." (Similarly, in Gaza, subliterate jihadis with an inadequate understanding of the Laws of Gravity frequently fire weapons into the air to celebrate a bold terrorist attack on elderly Holocaust survivors or a baby in a crib, and are maimed or killed when those rounds fall to earth into their hate-filled heads. Oopsie.)

Likewise, the relentless gun grabbers at an orchestrated Town Hall fire wild accusations and ugly invective at awesome NRA spokeswoman Dana Loesch, at President Trump, at any defenders of our constitutional right to keep and bear arms. And then they are completely taken aback when their arguments bounce off their intended targets and come back to hit them as their tissue of lies unravels. Turns out that the way Ms. Loesch was treated at CNN's Town Hall has been a great recruiting tool for NRA membership. Ping! Ow! Ricochet!

Two best-selling t-shirts at gun shows are "I carry a 9 mm because a cop is too heavy," and "When seconds count, the cops are minutes away." Never has a more heartbreaking illustration of the truth of the latter slogan come to light than in the recent horror show in Parkland, Florida.

An active shooter was on the rampage inside a school and we learned that a man sworn to protect and serve was hiding outside the building. Then we learned that there was not ONE man derelict in his duty, but FOUR. My husband and I have known many soldiers from many wars, and several fine officers of the law. Mr. AG said he simply does not believe that all four of those men were unwilling to run toward danger as all of our brave and selfless First Responders are taught to do. He believes it HAD to be an order handed down from some swamp dweller above their pay grade.

Perhaps from Democrat Sheriff David Israel himself who has bragged repeatedly that "the lion doesn't care about the opinions of the sheep." If I were Mr. Israel, I would be reluctant to call myself a "lion" lest it invoke the obvious comparison to the Cowardly Lion in Wizard of Oz. Just sayin'.

I believe that most of the parents would have run into the school with nothing but David's slingshot and five smooth stones if they thought they could divert fire away from their children and towards themselves.

And still the gun grabbers would love forcibly to confiscate our guns and abolish our right to self-defense. Do they honestly believe that this episode should inspire us to outsource our safety to Crouching Paper Tigers waiting somewhere safe until all the fuss dies down? Sheriff Israel – pausing briefly from screaming at Dana Loesch and the NRA – inadvertently let slip that what he needed was MORE power. Really? There's a catchy slogan: More power to cower! And this man still has a job?

Nikolas J. Cruz was a ticking time bomb almost from birth. In the totality of this Epic Fail, gun ownership is the least of it. If not a gun, it would have been a bomb, a truck, or arson. And legal gun ownership by anyone else on earth had absolutely nothing to do with it.

Most of the other factors in the Epic Fail besides the stand down of Law Enforcement cannot be said aloud. Let's start with Genetics, one of the biggest taboos of all. His birth mother did not even know who the father was. Let me just say that there is scarcely a family in America in which one young couple did not produce a baby fewer than 9 months after the wedding. But very few women are so promiscuous, irresponsible, or stupid that they have no idea who the father was. This woman arranged a private adoption with Cruz's long-suffering adoptive parents. With either a very long learning curve or as a business model, the woman then had a second child with a different father. This baby boy also was adopted by the Cruz family.

By age 3, Nikolas was diagnosed with developmental difficulties and shortly thereafter with the whole panoply of alphabet soup "disorders": ADHD, Emotional-Behavioral Disorder, Depression, Anxiety, Social Awkwardness. At 19, he had not yet graduated high school.

Let's move on from Genetics to misguided Social Justice Policy that came straight from Holder's DOJ and Obama. Because of the diversity industry's aversion to any racial disparity in school discipline – completely irrespective of who is actually causing the trouble! – it is likely that this pale kid with the last name of "Cruz" was not given the mental illness diagnosis or in-school arrests that would have kept legal guns out of his hands forever.

Finally, let's "have a conversation" about how the great Leviathan of agencies in place to monitor problems didn't just DROP the ball, they kicked it away like a soccer goalie. Dozens of people warned numerous agencies including the FBI about the shooter's bizarre and threatening behavior. In desperation, Cruz himself warned that he was distraught about his mother's death and losing control. The "if you see something, say something," popularized after 9/11, proved worse than useless. A chorus not much smaller than The Mormon Tabernacle Choir "said things and said things" to no avail. Reporting danger and being ignored is infinitely WORSE than not reporting at all. It leads the conscientious callers to believe that the problem is being solved, when nothing whatsoever has been done!

How then to address the problem of school shootings? To you gleeful potential gun grabbers: You go first! Turn in your ARs, your handguns, your knives, your baseball bats, your sharpened spoons. Throw in your fireplace pokers and frozen legs of lamb. Put up a mandatory sign outside your home advertising its morally superior quality: "Weapon-Free Zone. Not One Thing With Which to Defend Ourselves Inside!" What is holding you back?

In our over-55 development in Arizona, there are surely hundreds to thousands of weapons, including many AR-15s. In fact, when I attended a fundraising dinner for our county's sheriff, the raffle prize was an AR and sales lagged because everybody already had one. Had every single gun in our complex been turned in on February 13, it would have changed nothing in this or any other mass-murder disaster. Outside of a pigeon who committed suicide by bb gun next door, there has never been a shooting in our complex.

Harden the soft targets. Recruit vets and other volunteers proficient with firearms to help protect schools. Get serious about mental illness and repeat troublemakers without regard to quotas based on race. Hey, kids, colored or pale, here's a novel idea: if you don't want to be on the so-called school to prison fast track, don't be a damn criminal! Try the school to college track or the school to work track. It's really not all that hard. It's not our sacred duty to make it easier for you to repeatedly evade responsibility for your rotten and evil choices in life.

To whatever degree possible, make the corporate gun grabbers pay financially. Here is Mr. AG's final paragraph in his cancellation letter to LifeLock requesting a refund:

"In case you are wondering, this is in specific response to your severance of a business relationship you had with the N.R.A. One of the reasons I paid you these past years is that I expected that in case of an identity theft issue, you would be zealous and determined on my behalf. Since you caved on the N.R.A. issue, I expect that in case of genuine dispute over identity theft, you could cave on other issues as well, especially if someone can make them controversial. Moral cowardice renders an advocate worthless."

H. L. Mencken said: "For every complex problem, there is a solution that is clear, simple...and wrong." If he wasn't talking about gun control, he should have been.

OPTIONS IN LIFE

12 THINGS MORE ACCURATE THAN CNN

Pravda
Astrology
Fortune Cookies
The weight listed on your Driver's License.
Your car clock. Especially after Daylight Savings Time kicks in on Sunday.
A scaredy-cat liberal's first time shooting at a gun range.
The initial estimated budget for your daughter's wedding.
The wheat harvest projection in every Soviet 5-Year Plan.
The IPCC's global warming predictions from 10 years ago.
The Psychic Hot-Line
A bathroom scale accidentally heaved down the basement stairs.
2016 Presidential Polls on November 8. Never. Gets. Old.

10 THINGS OR PEOPLE FUNNIER THAN JIMMY KIMMEL

Mad Libs
A Kid with a Knock-Knock Joke Book on a Cross-Country Trip
Maxine Waters
Bazooka Joe comix in bubble gum
Marmaduke cartoons
Louis Farrakhan
Cher's Tweets
A Nancy Pelosi press conference
Barack Hussein Obama unplugged from his Teleprompter
Mr. Potato Head

20 SHADES OF BORING

This being five long long days since the Oscars, most things worth saying about that unwatched little trifle have already been said. I also did not watch. Mostly because I have rarely seen more than one or two of the wretched movies. Also, I cannot keep straight any of the indistinguishable little self-important actors pontificating about one thing or another — #OscarsSoWhite; #ProducersSoPiggish; #ElderlyWomenSoNotHired. Whatever.

As a public service, however, for next year's Oscars or any of the 37 other self-congratulatory awards shows in between, I am going to list 20 things you can do with that evening that will be more fulfilling, interesting, or fun. Some will be all three. Other suggestions welcome.

Trip to Ross (Dress for Less!) return line.

Pre-address your Christmas cards. Do not affix stamps. Some addressees could pass on by December.

Play "Concentration" with deck of playing cards and a 4-year old. Lose badly. Insist on grudge match.

Watch an old Castro speech. It will be shorter and less anti-American than most Oscar acceptance speeches and more humorous than Jimmy Kimmel.

Order a Gary Cooper, Kirk Douglas, Humphrey Bogart, James Garner or John Wayne movie and see what an actual man looked like in the Olden Days.

Find an old Oscar show from the Johnny Carson era and watch an elegant, funny host without a political agenda.

Knit a Woke Pussy Hat™ with little Angora testicles attached as earflaps to show you, like, totally understand that women are not the only ones who, like, have vaginas. As if.

Go to bed early and read in bed.
Go to bed early and do not read in bed. Something else could occur to you.
Count your ammo. Organize by caliber.
Count individual cartridges in boxes to make sure there really are 500.

Clean a closet. Organize clothes by size: Small with intention to fit into any day; Tight-Medium, not tried on in store; Comfortable, mainly muu-muus; and the Emergency Jeans of Shame in the back of the closet.

Drink. Especially if Jeans of Shame are getting snug. Drunk-dial your Congressperson, promising huge contribution. Never have empty mailbox again.
Under no circumstances should you make drunk threats to an elected official unless you are a Democrat. Then, of course, when confronted with the clear and obvious crime, say that magic eraser phrase, "I was joking." Works every time.

Read the Constitution. It's actually shockingly short. See if you can locate the penumbra where those wacky Founding Fathers supported baby killing.

Try to dance all the way through "In-A-Gadda-Da-Vida." Call chiropractor.
Try to jump rope indoors on Mexican tile. Schedule knee replacement surgery. Also order new lamp.
Call your mother if you are blessed to still have one.
Bake a pie from scratch. Contemplate where the hell the expression "easy as pie" came from.

Do yoga. When husband comes home from bar at 2 a.m., have him gently help you out of Full Lotus Position. Ask physician about BOGO rate on knee replacements.

SAVING DAYLIGHT

March 16, 2018

I hope by now you are more or less adjusted to Daylight Savings Time. I have read that it takes as long as a week for our body clocks to recover from "losing" that hour. (Try flying to Israel sometime…about the time your body knows what's going on, it's time to fly home.)

As you probably already know, I live in Arizona. Our State Motto is "Whatever the rest of you are doing, we don't feel like it." But when I lived in Minnesota, there was many the March social event at which Mr. AG and I showed up half an hour late the day Daylight Savings Time kicked in. And the reason we were only HALF an hour late was because I am routinely half an hour EARLY to everything. To Mr. AG's dismay and occasional embarrassment. It is not unheard of for our dinner hosts still to be in the shower when we ring the bell.

Sorry. I can't help it; it's just the way I was raised. On-time is "late." Either tell us things start half an hour later than they actually do, or shower earlier. Alternatively, you could simply invite someone less neurotically-prompt.

I realize early arrival can be annoying, but not NEARLY as annoying as perpetual tardiness. I have had to "break up with" a woman friend who routinely left me sitting at various restaurants in the Twin Cities for an hour before she would waltz in with some unsatisfyingly-vague excuse. She was a nice and interesting person, but I find it grotesquely uncomfortable to sit alone, waving off impatient waiters, nursing one tepid drink, memorizing the lunch menu and fending off attractive men who ask if you are waiting for someone.

Okay, not only did that last thing never happen, but this was long before Smartphones, when you have a ready-made companion to fiddle with, not only while you wait, but even long after your lunch date appears. Sheesh! It is common now to see whole families out to dinner, each on his or her own phone, paying no attention whatsoever to each other. Sad.

Meanwhile, back at our topic which, if memory serves me, was saving daylight. As you no doubt know, Arizona does not do DST. The last thing on God's green earth that Arizona needs from March through October is another hour of blazing sunshine.

This means that now when I wish to speak with my 92-year-old father in Assisted Living in Minnesota, I have an even more difficult time trying to find a time to call. I must be both awake and fully caffeinated. And I must hit that small window when he is not either in the dining room or napping. After just 17 or 18 rings, he hears the phone over Fox News and picks up. He is, thank God, still in possession of all of his faculties and far more articulate than, say, Nancy Pelosi or Maxine Waters, though admittedly that is a low bar. But he is about as loquacious as Calvin Coolidge was reputed to be. So we have a two- or three-minute conversation about what he ate for breakfast, politics, and the weather, say we love each other and call it a day.

(Bonus Cal Coolidge joke: President and Mrs. Coolidge are at a Country Fair in Iowa. The First Lady's party is at an exhibit in which there are several chickens and a rooster. The pitchman tries to embarrass the First Lady. "Madame, did you know that the rooster does his duty up to 20 times a day?" She graciously takes it in stride, "Well, I must tell the

President." They move on. Later in the day, the President's party and Mrs. Coolidge's group meet up at the same exhibit. Mrs. Coolidge repeats the factoid she has just learned, "Dear, this gentleman says that the rooster does his duty up to 20 times a day." And without missing a beat, "Silent Cal" asks, "Same chicken?")

I remember as a kid hearing the farmers expressing great hatred for changing the time twice a year. I know very little about farming except that it's really hard physical work and I don't want to do it. I have admiration bordering on awe for those who do. Evidently dairy cows do not automatically get with the program. As a former nursing mother, I get it.

Golfers and country clubs like DST — mothers trying to get kids to bed in the summer, less so. We used to play outdoors until you couldn't see the ball, which ball depended on the season. For modern children, "the outdoors" is that brief airy space between Mom's car and the Mall where they can buy the latest games for their phones, computers and electronic devices.

Though I thought Mrs. Obama's All Kale-All the Time school lunch disaster was misguided, I had a certain amount of sympathy for her "Play 60" initiative in which various celebrity athletes tried to get kids off their lard butts to run around for an hour. It is quite horrifying to contemplate needing a formal program to convince young children to run around and play. But evidently, that's where we are now.

When I was a kid growing up in the '50s, we were routinely tossed outside at first light into the elements of whatever season we were in and forced to find our own fun with bikes, skates, jump ropes, hula hoops, toy guns, rocks, and sports equipment, some of it improvised.

We played many death-defying games that, if the Authorities

discovered kids playing them today, would cause the parents to be sentenced to reeducation camps or prison: Oh, not just Tag or Dodgeball, which are universally forbidden in every school now. I mean Crack the Whip (long line of skaters going fast, holding hands, with small skater on end learning about centrifugal force.); Red Rover (two lines of kids holding hands, a member from one line running full-speed at weakest link of opposite line. Game ends with first dislocated shoulder); King of the Hill (one person on top of a berm or dirt-pile from new house being built; object is to dislodge that person and occupy hill for brief time. Game ends with first broken collar bone). We won't even discuss Kill The Man With the Ball.

Daylight Savings Time, in those wonderful endless summers of our childhood, extended the days, and forced our mothers to call us in many more times. Exhausted Moms would employ the nearly-serious "Middle Name Call" – Susan Marie!! — and then, eventually, resort to The Dreaded Plan D – for Daddies calling. Uh-oh. Gotta go!

As painful as it is to lose that hour, don't worry, it will be back November 4th. According to Wikipedia, despite our best intentions, we never seem to take that luxurious extra hour of sleep. Maybe this year, we can use that extra hour to help get out the vote for the election two days later. Turn that much ballyhooed Blue Wave into a new Red Sea.

IT'S THE ARROGANCE, STUPID!

March 23, 2018

"All of a sudden white women, who were going to vote for me and frankly standing up to the men in their lives and the men in their workplaces, were being told, 'She's going to jail. You don't want to vote for her. It's terrible, you can't vote for that.' So, it just stopped my momentum…I was winning, and I thought I had fought my way back in the ten days from that letter until the election. I fell a little bit short." Hillary Rodham Clinton, Participation Trophy Candidate for President and current mental patient.

Hillary, seriously, we can't take much more. Reach deep down and find a little dignity. Apparently, nobody told you the Deplorable Speech probably lost you ten million votes. Minimum. Let's see if the Dumb Racist Red States Full of Idiot White Women Speech can outdo that! Let us count all the ways in which you are wrong. Or most of them – I only have so much time in my day before I have to trudge whitely into the kitchen in my bare feet to make food for my husband, lest he beat me.

Okay, first of all, you arrogant snot, you did not fall "a little bit" short in your second run at the Presidency; Trump ate your lunch. Where you fell was into your van and right after delivering these shameful remarks in a foreign country, you almost fell downstairs. Twice. And then you fractured your wrist allegedly falling in the bathtub because the negligent Indians failed to force two burly toxic males to stand by to forklift you out of the tub. That would be some tough duty with a high rate of PTSD.

Secondly, maybe you haven't heard, but there's a SECRET ballot. All those intimidated, empty-headed white women could vote however they pleased – their icky spouses and male workmates be damned.

Thirdly, here's the truth, Mrs. Clinton, and, if no one else will say it, I will: as some sort of shining example of a white woman "standing up to the men in their lives," you are a total, pathetic failure. Gennifer Flowers wasn't enough to kick Bill to the curb? Cigars in the Oval Office with a woman six years older than Chelsea didn't frost your cupcake? "You better put some ice on that!" ring any bells? Five trips on The Lolita Express? You are STILL married to the bum, for the love of Pete. Yeah, GREAT "standing up," kiddo. And you had the temerity to mock Tammy Wynette for "Stand By Your Man"?

A lot of women stick with hounds because they have no choice – no money, a bunch of kids and no prospects. You have a law degree, and half of marital assets totaling a billion dollars, give or take. But you needed Bill's clout to continue your Long Shoeless Lurch to the top of the political heap.

The women who DID vote for you do not need to "stand up to the men in their lives" because most don't have any men in their lives. Who is your base, besides hard-core leftists? A lot of single women, including unmarried mothers who consider Big Sugar Daddy Welfare (taxpayers, really) to be their man. Women with other women as their partners. Celebrities who change partners as often as they change movie roles. Self-important harridans married to wussie sorta-men who barely count as males.

We married white women were totally enamored of you until we "were being told" that you were going to jail? So you are saying that we married white women don't follow Twitter or navigate the Internet or read the newspapers or watch TV to get our news? We just sit there looking pretty and pale until we are "told" by our menfolk what to think. I've never heard anything more sexist from a MAN.

Although you could be right, because I have no opinions, no issues I care about until I get my marching orders from Mr. AG. He assures me that we BOTH care about secure borders, vetted fake refugees, vetted fake Dreamers, Israel, free speech, religious freedom and Second Amendment rights. You were 0 for 7 on those. You opposed Voter I.D. You were too cowardly to say "All Lives Matter." You favor abortion up until labor pains are 3 minutes apart, possibly beyond. And we haven't even gotten to Benghazi, uranium saleswoman of the month, or your personal qualities yet.

I was NEVER going to vote for you. NEVER. I didn't even like you when I was a Democrat.

George W. Bush said after candidate Trump's attacks on "low-energy Jeb!" that "Donald, you can't insult your way to the Presidency." That turned out to be wrong. But, Hillary, you would do well to heed that advice. You can't insult half the ELECTORATE to a third bite at the apple. Oh, how we wish you could! I would love to see President Trump (how that must rankle to see that in print every day...) take you on again. And I especially would love to see a real down-and-dirty catfight in the Democratic primary – you and Bernie and Kamala and the Indian Maiden on the Land O' Lakes Butter Box – all scratching and biting and hissing for the right to see who will lose to The Donald again. Popcorn City!

One would think that these wretched remarks about white women would constitute the low point of your analysis of how you lost the election. But one would be wrong. These were nothing compared to the boring, repetitive, infuriating slander that Red State residents are racists. And Unreliable Confused Racists, at that, who voted TWICE for that Black guy you lost to and then suddenly smacked their foreheads and remembered that they were bigots. Though how voting for the OTHER white person in the race constitutes "racism" is a real poser. Nice touch, also, to claim that Red Staters hate East Indians. Your Indian audience might have heard of Nikki Haley, who has a much better chance of being the first woman President than you do.

Boy, is your shtick getting old, lady. Plus, I just have to say that whoever you have now as a Wardrobe Consultant must be a vicious plant from Ivanka's fashion house. I did not think it was possible to find a more unflattering garment than that carpet remnant pants suit. But the billowy maternity dress over the pedal pushers beat that all hollow. Cultural appropriation, anyone? What's next – hoop earrings? (Run, kids! Find your PlayDoh and plush toys!) Hillary, I am going to end with a humane plea, a prayer, for you to stop humiliating yourself, take up a hobby – you seem a natural for snow-boarding — and enjoy your grandchildren.

Let me express it more elegantly by plagiarizing. I say, if one is going to plagiarize, one should steal from the best. I offer to Hillary the severely-truncated words of Oliver Cromwell in his speech to the House of Commons – April 20, 1653 – on the occasion of the Dissolution of the Long Parliament. It's been 365 years, and I can no way improve on it. I am also taking the liberty of changing the plural aimed at the members of Parliament into the singular aimed at Mrs. Clinton. Oliver, forgive me; it's in a good cause!

"Ye are a mercenary wretch, and would, like Esau sell your country for a mess of pottage, and like Judas betray your God for a few pieces of money....ye are grown intolerably odious to the whole nation. You have sat too long for any good you have been doing lately... Depart, I say; and let us have done with you. In the name of God, go!"

THE COLUMN TURNS FOUR

March 30, 2018

Holy Moly, Rocky, what a Big Deal Day! Today at sunset begins the first night of Passover; it is also Good Friday; and, the 4th anniversary of the Thoughts From the Ammo Line column!

In the old Electric Company song, we learned "Two of these things belong together, two of these things are kind of the same. But, one of these things doesn't belong here..." Okay, the column is not up there with the Flight to Freedom from Egypt or the Crucifixion. Let us just stipulate to that. It's like saying that Rhode Island is the 3rd biggest state out of Alaska, Texas, and Rhode Island. True, as far as it goes, but misleading.

Since I have never missed a week – neither sloth nor indolence nor dark of night nor ache of head after an adult beverage or two has kept me from my appointed rounds – that means that I have helped kick off your weekends for 208 straight Fridays. It has been my privilege, thanks be to all four Power Line Boys, and a source of great joy for me. Many of you have been kind to remark that you look forward to the columns and that they bring you a small respite from a sad and difficult world, and I have to assure you – again –that you faithful readers and erudite, amusing, regular commenters make MY day, too! Every. Single. Week!

I must especially thank Scott, my friend and dedicated editor, who has spared me many a humiliation in lack of agreement between subject and predicate, and also has spared you dear readers from a few – but only a few – puerile and tasteless jokes. Sadly, the kind I am most drawn to. Most of the time Scott lets me skate on the thin ice; a couple of times he has said, in so many words, "Uh, not on my watch." Of course, more elegant and lawyerly than that. "I must counsel you that that was beneath you."

In taking personal stock over the last 208 weeks, it has been a time of incredible highs (our son's wedding, gaining a ready-made grandson), and the lowest of lows with my beloved mother's passing. I have lost 40 pounds! More accurately, four separate, crabby times in those four years I have lost that "last" 10 lbs! And regained it within minutes.

I tore a rotator cuff that has almost recovered to, maybe, 70 percent. I am pretty much resigned to the fact that this will be as good as it gets. I plinked in the desert last week and was only able to fire about 250 rounds before my arm and shoulder got fatigued enough to impact accuracy. Many deal with so much worse; I am not complaining. If I am ever in a gun battle that requires more than 250 rounds, it would be a sign that things are not going to end at all well.

I have made several sets of friends from the column – Abby and Ken in Florida; and Mark and Becky in Prescott, Arizona, where we "summer," and also one set with access to very fancy seats at the Diamondbacks. Not that they wouldn't be friends without that. But it can't hurt. Plus, I feel that about 100 of you are now "family." I worry when you don't appear!

The Cubs have won the World Series and so did the Houston Astros (hometown favorite of young Brody and Brielle who have yet to learn that the entire point of professional sports is to break your heart!), and Donald J. Trump won the Presidency in the biggest, most historic upset in my lifetime. The ensuing Tsunami of Derangement will provide columns forever.

Ironically enough, the original impetus for this column – my standing in line at Walmart for hundreds of hours during the Great Obama Ammo Drought – has evaporated with President Trump's election. Ah, humans, especially Americans! When we think something is going to be taken away from us, we try to hoard. When the immediate threat is gone, we feel we can relax. With the election of a President who spoke to the NRA convention, everyone had temporarily relaxed and sales were off to a significant degree. The ammo shelves are full.

But know this: the gun control despots will NEVER give up, as we can see with the well-financed Brain-Dead Blathering Teen Tour.

What IS IT with these scrawny little future tyrants and their sexual imagery? Young muscle-free Mr. Hogg talking about elected officials being "the NRA'S bitches" and childish Mr. Colbert smirking about "c*ckholsters" for Putin. Get some therapy, boys. Or at least some manners.

Obama fantasized aloud about "a million" Obama clones. (Maybe he recently saw "Boys From Brazil" on Netflix...) Well, sir, to quote Sondheim's "Send in the Clowns": Don't bother, they're here!: the left-wing indoctrination factories masquerading as schools in all 57 of our states have easily churned out a million lazy, pompous, intolerant bullies and thin-skinned busybodies, long on unwarranted self-esteem and woefully short on knowledge or even curiosity.

My friends, we cannot get demoralized or discouraged. We have to fight. Make it your mission to get at least one new person to join the NRA. Consider becoming a Life Member or making an extra donation to its Legal Fund. Cede NOTHING. I do not want to hear about, I do not want to read about, I do not want you even to THINK: "Oh woe is us; the midterms are lost!" The midterms are seven long months away. If we can't defeat these potty-mouthed little Tide Pod Snackers, we truly are lost as a nation. We must be the "winter soldiers" of Valley Forge. Watch the "John Adams"series or "D-Day" to grasp what was bequeathed to us in sacrifice.

Happy Passover! Happy Easter! God Bless America where we can celebrate religious freedom, freedom of speech (both of which the Left also hates and opposes) and the Second Amendment which underwrites all our other freedoms. Courage! Never give up.

AFTERWORD

And thus ends Volume 4 of the compilation columns from Thoughts From the Ammo Line. Thank you for buying the book, reading the book, and giving it a nice little 5-Star Review on Amazon. That really helps a lot. But, mostly, whether or not you agree with every word of every column, thank you for being the kind of person who takes our precious, Constitutionally-guaranteed freedoms of speech and self-defense seriously.

The previous 3 volumes are:

Volume 1, *Ammo Grrrll Hits the Target*
Volume 2, *Ammo Grrrll Aims True*
Volume 3, *Ammo Grrrll Returns Fire*

Own them all – lined up in a pretty, colorful row on your most visible bookshelf. Or in the bathroom.

Watch for Volume 5, *Ammo Grrrll: Straight Shooter*, due out in summer of 2019.

Also watch for anything by her famous novelist husband, Max Cossack. He also appreciates 5-Star reviews on Amazon. His books are really really entertaining. Hey, if you can't trust the word of a WIFE, for heaven's sake, whose can you trust?

Thanks again.

Written this 30th day of March, 2019
Susan Vass